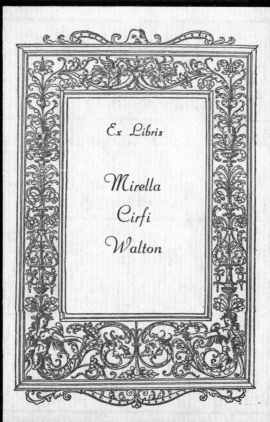

The MIT Press

Cambridge, Massachusetts

London, England

Socrates' Ancestor

An Essay on Architectural Beginnings

Indra Kagis McEwen

© 1993 Massachusetts Institute of Technology

All rights reserved. No part of this book may be reproduced in any form by any electronic or mechanical means (including photocopying, recording, or information storage and retrieval) without permission in writing from the publisher. This book was set in Perpetua by DEKR Corporation and was printed and bound in the United States of America.

Library of Congress Cataloging-in-Publication Data

McEwen, Indra Kagis.

    Socrates' ancestor : an essay on architectural beginnings / Indra Kagis McEwen.

      p.   cm.

    Originally presented as the author's thesis (Master—McGill University School of Architecture).

    Includes bibliographical references and index.

    ISBN 0-262-13292-3. — ISBN 0-262-63148-2 (pbk.)

    1. Architecture—Greece.   2. Architecture—Philosophy.   I. Title.

NA270.M38   1993

722'.8—dc20   93-21863

                                              CIP

À Jean, Jean-Sabin, Marianne et Jérémie

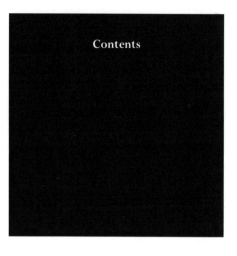

Contents

Preface

The horizon recedes as we approach it.

It is perhaps therefore inevitable that the near recklessness of undertaking to explore a territory as vast as the one I have ventured into has meant broaching more questions than I have answered. To those who helped me avoid losing myself entirely, I owe my thanks.

To Alberto Pérez-Gómez, for his trust in my earliest intuitions, and for his support when this essay first took shape as a master's thesis in the History and Theory Program at the McGill University School of Architecture.

To Joseph Rykwert, for his patience in reading and discussing work in progress, for his encouragement, and for his many valuable suggestions and remarks.

To Marco Frascari, Donald Kunze, and David Leatherbarrow for early guidance.

To George Hersey and Robert Jan van Pelt for their enthusiasm.

To the anonymous classics scholar whose careful reading of the manuscript steered me clear of many pitfalls.

To my mother, Yvette Kagis, for help with German sources.

To the staff of the McGill Library Systems, especially the Interlibrary Loans Department at the McLennan Library, for their kind cooperation with my (always urgent) requests.

To the Classics Department at McGill for allowing me access to Ibycus, and to Anne Carson and Margaret Contogiorgis for help with Greek.

To Sarah P. Morris for her generosity in releasing proofs of her *Daidalos and the Origins of Greek Art* to me when its publication was delayed.

To Roger Conover at the MIT Press for his unfailing support and to Matthew Abbate for sensitive editing.

To my friend Judith Terry for expert proofreading assistance.

And finally, to Geoffrey James for the cover photograph that so aptly ensnares these fugitive thoughts.

I have used standard, albeit occasionally emended, translations of the classical authors, relying principally on the Loeb Classical Library. The transliteration of Greek words follows accepted usage with, as I fear, the usual inconsistencies.

Montreal
January 1993

Geoffrey James,
"The Museum of the Villa Adriana, 1989."

I

Introduction:
Socrates' Ancestor

In Plato's dialogue *Euthyphro*, where Socrates questions Euthyphro, who is prosecuting his own father for murder, on the nature of holiness and unholiness, of piety and impiety, justice and injustice, Socrates succeeds, as he so often does, in completely confusing his interlocutor.

Euthyphro: *I really do not know, Socrates, how to express what I mean. For somehow or other our arguments, on whatever ground we rest them, seem to turn round and walk away from us.*

Socrates: *Your words, Euthyphro, are like the handiwork of my ancestor Daedalus; and if I were the sayer or propounder of them, you might say that my arguments walk away and will not remain fixed because I am a descendent of his. . . . [For your] notions . . . show an inclination to be on the move. . . .*

Euthyphro: *Nay, Socrates, I shall still say that you are the Daedalus who sets arguments in motion; not I, certainly, but you make them move or go round. . . .*

Socrates: *Then I must be greater than Daedalus: for whereas he only made his own inventions to move, I move those of other people as well. And the beauty of it is, that I would rather not. For I would give the wisdom of Daedalus [**Daidalou sophia**] . . . to be able to detain them and keep them fixed.*[1]

The year is 399 B.C. Socrates and Euthyphro both await judiciary hearings: Euthyphro to lay the charge against his father, Socrates to be charged for corrupting the youth of Athens. They converse before the stoa in the agora. Beyond them rises the Athenian acropolis, bright with the newly com-

pleted structures of the century that has just ended: the Pro-
pylaea, the Erectheion, the temple of Nike Apteros, and, of
course, the Parthenon, temple of the city and its emblem,
where, as many have noted, sculpture and architecture converge to the point where to distinguish them becomes not only
impossible but irrelevant.

In the career of Daedalus,[2] as in the Parthenon, sculpture
and architecture also converge, for Daedalus, considered the
mythical first architect, built not only the automata referred
to in this passage, but also the Labyrinth and the *choros*,[3] or
dancing-floor, at Knossos as well as a fortified city in Sicily.
Socrates, whose father Sophroniskos was a *lithourgos*, a stone-
mason or stone carver[4] (once more the line between building
and sculpting is blurred), claims Daedalus as his ancestor,[5] and
in so doing suggests—not without irony, derision being a
familiar undercurrent of the Socratic tone[6]—the existence of
an ancestral blood tie between architecture and philosophy,
between the creations of Daedalus and speculative thought.

To explore the nature of this tie is the purpose of this
inquiry. Why does it seem important to do so?

For the past century, the dawn of Western thought—
considered in the twentieth-century twilight of its apparent
decline—the "discovery of the mind," as Bruno Snell has called
it, the "theoretical event" or "birth of spiritual Europe" in
Husserl's terms, has been the subject of intensive study. Much
of the discussion, to which philosophers, cultural historians,
classical philologists, and anthropologists have all contributed,
has naturally focused on the culture of archaic Greece and on
the thought of the pre-Socratic philosophers. One approach,
whose hidden agenda has been a systematic secularization, has
concentrated on tracing pre-Socratic thought first to mythical,

then to ritual or tribal roots. For all the brilliance of its scholarship, this is an approach that has tended to result in a "nothing but" kind of assessment, of which F. M. Cornford's *From Religion to Philosophy*[7] is an important early example: an assessment that ultimately begs the very questions it purports to answer. To attempt to eliminate the mystery of human existence by reducing its articulations in myth and speculation to the evolutionary products of "nothing but" tribal custom still leaves unaccounted for the mystery at the very core of tribal custom itself.

If this line of thinking has dealt with the emergence of Western thought by tracing supposed effect back to supposed evolutionary cause, another line of thinking has concentrated on the phenomenon of emergence, the event, itself. To this second school belong thinkers such as Heidegger and the philosopher of history Eric Voegelin.[8] For them, especially in their later work, the essential thing has been to preserve the mystery of human existence against erosion by "nothing but," through a study of the pre-Socratics that has had as its chief aim the disclosure of early Greek thinking as the West's first articulation of that mystery *as* a mystery. This disclosure not only mitigates the picture of early Greek thinkers as either highly evolved tribesmen on the one hand or as underdeveloped nuclear physicists on the other, this last, to oversimplify matters, being the second half of the Cornford kind of argument; it also reveals fresh possibilities for being in the present twilight. For if the assessment of the first Greek thinkers as tribesmen/physicists has affirmed, and even encouraged, the scientism of this century, then disclosure of the awareness of mystery inherent in the articulations of emerging Greek thought suggests an alternative affirmation.

Plato, in the *Euthyphro*, suggests a link between architecture and such thought. It would be not only foolish but pointless to interpret this link as evolutionary or causal, to claim that architecture, taken as the embodiment of ritual,[9] gave rise to philosophy, and so to fall into the "nothing but tribal custom" trap. Rather, as I shall argue, the awareness embodied in the architectural beginnings of archaic Greece shares a blood tie with the awareness that first becomes explicit in the speculative thought of the sixth century B.C. As equivalent manifestations of an emerging Western consciousness, the "architectural event," if it may be so called, and the "theoretical event" can be understood as related moments in a single occurrence. It is of particular interest that the architectural event, chronologically speaking, came first, not so much because the roots of Greek thinking are to be unearthed in Greek architecture as such, but because, if the consciousness that is the hallmark of Husserl's "spiritual Europe" first appeared in architecture, it is perhaps in this (first, architectural) moment of the emergence of Western consciousness that the possibilities for alternative affirmations are most readily revealed.

In the passage cited earlier, Socrates sets arguments in motion, just as, according to legend, his ancestor Daedalus had set statues in motion. But Socrates' most ardent wish is to keep them still: he "would give the wisdom of Daedalus . . . to be able to detain them and keep them fixed." This is a fifth-century aspiration, and the distance from the dawn of Greek thought is already considerable. In the *Hippias Major*,[10] where Socrates says that the sculptors of his day would ridicule the works that earned Daedalus his fame, the inference is that moving statues are silly, just as in the passage cited the inference is that Euthyphro's circular arguments are silly. Knowledge is at odds with things that will not stay put, as a passage in the *Meno*,[11] where Socrates once more evokes the creations of his ancestor, confirms:

Meno: . . . *I wonder that knowledge [**epistēmē**] should be preferred to right opinion [**doxa**]—or why they should even differ.*
. . . .

Socrates: *You would not wonder if you had ever observed the images of Daedalus . . . [which] require to be fastened in order to keep them, and if they are not fastened they will play truant and run away. . . . I mean to say that they are not very valuable possessions if they are at liberty, for they will walk off like runaway slaves; but when fastened, they are of great value, for they are really beautiful works of art. . . . When they are bound, in the first place, they have the nature of knowledge; and in the second place, they are abiding. And this is why knowledge is more honourable and excellent than true opinion, because fastened by a chain.*

As Françoise Frontisi-Ducroux has observed in her penetrating study of the Daedalus legend, the expedient of binding these primitive Daedalean statues [**xoana**] with cords or chains was a way of making the divine life in them manifest.[12] Motion was life, and the animated life, the very divinity, of these images was best revealed by tying them down. For Plato, divinity, insofar as knowledge had divinity as its source and object, lay in fixity, and Plato's emphasis was on the bound state as such. In the culture of prephilosophical Greece, divinity lay in animation, and **xoana** were bound not because the fixed object was divine in its fixity, but rather the opposite. The emphasis was on the unbound, the animated state: the chains that bound the cult statue harnessed a fearful, excessive, super-natural life only in order to better disclose its presence.

The contrast here made is somewhat subtler than I have so far suggested it to be. In the case of Daedalus' *xoana*, the chaining of cult statues brought the divine into the realm of human experience; for Plato, the binding of true opinion with the chains of recollection [*anamnēsis*][13] brings the divine into the realm of human knowledge. Plato's evocation of the animated cult statue reveals a detectable shift. In both cases binding has as its purpose to bring the divine into the human sphere, but there is a shift, and the shift is a shift of emphasis from the primacy of motion to the primacy of fixity; from the primacy of experience to the primacy of the knowledge Plato calls *epistēmē*.

Between the two poles of movement and of fixity, of experience and of knowledge, lies the phenomenon of the emerging Western consciousness, and to it, as Plato himself seems to suggest, the Daedalus story holds an important key. But, as already noted, Plato and his overt concern for fixity are already some distance from the earliest articulations of Greek speculative thought, and it is to the only verbatim record of the very first such articulation that I would now like to turn. A discussion of Daedalus and his legendary creations will come after, to be followed in turn by a discussion of the emergence of the *polis* and of the peripteral temple.

II

Anaximander
and the
Articulation of Order

Anaximander of Miletus,[1] second after Thales of the so-called Ionian naturalists (*physiologoi*), is generally looked upon as the first real philosopher and his thought as the watershed in the transition from myth to philosophy, the transition whereby a so-called rational account of the world takes the place of a so-called irrational one. Although Thales preceded Anaximander, and was, it is said, his teacher, Thales is seen more as a legendary sage[2] than a speculative thinker. The distinction is a slightly arbitrary one, however, cast as it is in the light of the modern disciplinary view of philosophy. Not only Thales but Anaximander too seems to have been active politically and architecturally as well as speculatively, for if Thales once changed the course of a river[3] and was active in promoting Ionian unity,[4] Anaximander, as I shall argue, built architectural models, and is said to have led a Milesian colonizing expedition to Apollonia on the Black Sea. Nevertheless, in the case of Anaximander, it is possible to piece together a cosmology— the very first Western cosmology—from Aristotle and the various commentaries, and this is something that simply cannot be done in the case of Thales. Moreover, although he has been credited with the authorship of a navigational treatise,[5] not one word of Thales' own survives. For Anaximander, on the other hand, we have the B1 fragment[6] from Simplicius' fifth-century A.D. commentary on the *Physics* of Aristotle, a fragment which, depending on how it is read, contains at least seventeen or at most fifty-six Greek words attributable to Anaximander himself. These seventeen to fifty-six words, coupled with the cosmology extrapolated from the commentaries, give a potentially coherent picture of Anaximander's world view, although it is one that continues to depend heavily on imaginative interpretation.

Charles H. Kahn's study of Anaximander cites Anaximander B1 in a somewhat longer form than usual, including more of Simplicius' surrounding text because, as he rightly argues, the quotation needs all the contextual help available for a proper interpretation. Kahn also argues convincingly that the direct quotation from Anaximander (even allowing for the Aristotelian interpolations of Simplicius) is fifty-six words in length, rather than the traditional seventeen, and begins after "he says that [*legei*]," instead of beginning with the usual "according to necessity [*kata to chreōn*]." This is Kahn's translation for the passage he cites. For reasons that should become clear in due course, I shall later propose an amended reading for the embedded direct quotation.

*Anaximander . . . declared the Boundless [**to apeiron**] to be the principle [**archē**] and element [**stoicheion**] of existing things [**ta onta**], having been the first to introduce this very term of "principle" [**archē**]. He says that [**legei**] "it is neither water nor any other of the so-called elements, but some different, boundless nature [**hetera tis physis apeiros**], from which all the heavens [**ouranoi**] arise and the **kosmoi** within them; out of those things [**ex hōn de**] whence is the generation for existing things [**ta onta**], into these [**eis tauta**] again does their destruction take place, according to what needs must be [**kata to chreōn**]; for they make amends and give reparation to one another for their offense, according to the ordinance of time [**kata tēn tou chronou taxin**]," speaking of them thus in rather poetical terms. It is clear that having observed the change of the four elements into one another he did not think it fit to make any one of these the material substratum, but something else besides these.*[7]

As Kahn points out, the traditional reading of the fragment, from Aëtius in the sixth century, through Nietzsche and Diels in the nineteenth, to Burnet in the twentieth, has been that the Boundless (*to apeiron*) of the first part of the passage is the source out of which (*ex hōn*), in the second part of the passage, existing things come to be, and into which (*eis tauta*) they also pass away, having made amends and given reparation to one another for their wrongdoing, "according to the ordinance of time." However, in this century it has been noted by Gregory Vlastos,[8] among others, that the *ex hōn*, the "out of which," that introduces the second part of the passage is in the plural, whereas *to apeiron*, its alleged referent, is singular. This led Vlastos to postulate the Boundless as something "explicitly thought of as a plurality . . . a compound of opposites,"[9] which is difficult to make sense of both grammatically and speculatively. In a later article, and presumably as a direct consequence of this thinking, Vlastos makes Anaximander's *apeiron*, for him the limitless fund of a plurality of undifferentiated stuff and the source of differentiated "existing things," into the speculative equivalent of Hesiod's *Chaos*,[10] which he also reads as an undifferentiated mixture. Vlastos has tended to oversimplify the issue. *Chaos*, whose coming to be (*genesis*) in Hesiod's *Theogony* precedes the coming to be of Earth (*Gaia*) and Heaven (*Ouranos*),[11] is not necessarily a mixture but appears to have been thought of as primordial gap.[12] Moreover if, as Aristotle says, *to apeiron* "encompasses and steers all things,"[13] its nature would appear to be at odds with that of Hesiodic *Chaos*, whether it is taken as a mixture or a gap. In any event, the identification of causal or evolutionary antecedents seldom brings one closer to a real understanding. But if *to apeiron* is not the referent for the relative pronoun *hōn* in the passage from Simplicius, if the Boundless is not what is referred to by the plural "which" out of which is the generation of existing things, what *does* the *hōn* refer to?

Kahn argues that *hōn* refers not to *to apeiron* but to *ta onta*, the existing things themselves. These, he says, are not, as they have often been taken to be, individual beings, such as men and animals. Nor, he claims, are *ta onta* the hypostatized, Aristotelian four elements Simplicius refers to at the conclusion of the passage, although Simplicius' evocation of the "change of the four elements into one another" does indeed help to elucidate Anaximander's intentions. As Kahn reads the passage, *ta onta* refers to the elemental qualities of hot, moist, cold, and dry, and even more generally to the changing seasons, as well as (by extension) to all natural cycles of birth, death, and regeneration. To extend Kahn's argument further, for Anaximander, *ta onta* are the "existing things" of experience, *as* experienced. Their ceaseless cyclical movement (*aidios kinēsis*), whereby hot dies into cold and cold, in turn, into warm; moist into dry, and vice versa; the seed into the earth, which once more generates seed; day into night, which dies into another dawn; and summer into winter, which expires at the inception of a new season of growth—these, collectively, are the generation and destruction "according to what needs must be [*kata to chreōn*]" referred to in the fragment. They, the *onta* of experience, "make amends and give reparation to one another for their offense, according to the ordinance [*taxis*— which has also been translated as "assessment" or "order"] of time." Kahn's argument reflects an understanding of the qualitative, compact experience of a mythical world still untouched by the differentiating, Aristotelian classifications that color all the commentaries, including Simplicius'. According to Kahn's analysis, the fragment makes no mention of things being generated out of, or by, the *apeiron*. Furthermore, he gives a very credible account of Anaximander's cosmos[14] as rooted in experience both of the natural and of the political order: a "universe governed by law," as he puts it.

I think Kahn is mistaken about the referent for the key word *hōn*, however. What his analysis of the grammar does is to split the direct quotation in half. With *ta onta* as the referent for *hōn*, the part that begins *ex hōn* and ends *kata tēn tou chronou taxin*, and deals with the qualitative elements that die into one another, becomes completely self-referential, with no connection to the first part of the passage: to the part that postulates "some different, boundless nature [*hetera tis physis apeiros*], from which all the heavens arise and the *kosmoi* within them." That there should be no connection between these two parts is extremely unlikely, especially since the two parts of the quotation are not even separated by a full stop but only by a half stop (transliterated as a semicolon).

Rather, I would venture, the *hōn* refers to *kosmoi*, the plural noun immediately preceding it in the passage. If so, the following would be the sense of Simplicius' citation.

The *archē* ("beginning," not Aristotelian "material principle") of all the elements (qualitative, not hypostatized, as Simplicius inevitably understands them) is not one of these elements themselves, but some different boundless nature (*hetera tis physis apeiros*), from which all the heavens (*ouranoi*) arise, and the *kosmoi* (orders) within these heavens. *And*—the inclusion of the particle *de* signals a connection with what goes before—out of these *kosmoi* is the generation *for*, not *of*, existing things,[15] and into these existing things destruction takes place according to what needs must be, for they (existing things, *onta*) make amends and give reparation to one another for their wrongdoing (*adikia*) according to the order of time.

With *kosmoi* taken as the referent for *hōn*, the whole passage attains a new coherence. Some boundless nature (*physis*) different from nature as the quality of experience,[16] some *other physis*, gives rise to the heavens and the *kosmoi* within the heavens. It is these "orders," generated by a boundless source which, as is elsewhere attested, is all-encompassing and divine, that regulate and guide the ebb and flow of elements experienced as things coming to be and passing away. This other, boundless *physis* is the generation for the *orders* of *onta*. It does not generate "existing things" themselves because, as Anaximander stresses, generation and destruction take place *kata to chreōn*, according to what needs must be, or, as Heidegger in his exegesis of Anaximander B1 translates it, "along the lines of usage."[17]

Now, a phrase that occurs frequently in Homer is *kata kosmon*, according to order, but it is always qualified, either as *ou* (not) *kata kosmon*: disorderly; or *eu* (well) *kata kosmon*:[18] orderly. In the very form of the phrase there resides an implicit assumption of some unnamed standard by which orderliness can be attributed to things, a measure by which things are "well" according to order or "not" according to order. This Homeric *kosmos* helps to elucidate Anaximander's *kata to chreōn*, while also expanding the sense of the entire passage.

The *kosmoi*, orders, that regulate generation and destruction regulate them inasmuch as *kosmoi* are the measures by which the flux of qualitative *onta* can be called well or ill ordered. These *kosmoi* do not control or determine ebb and flow, since in the *onta* of experience ebb and flow are often disorderly, as the mention of their *adikia* (wrongdoing, disorderliness) in the very next phrase of the passage stresses. Anaximander claims that out of *kosmoi* is the *genesis* (coming to be) for existing things, and "into the foregoing" (*eis tauta*, referring collectively to *kosmoi, ouranoi,* and *tis physis apeiros*)[19] destruction takes place *kata to chreōn*. It is the polysemic *chreōn* of need/necessity/custom/usage, itself a feature of experience and rooted firmly in the human sphere, that discloses *kosmoi* as the *genesis* for *onta*, and it is this that brings Heidegger's exploration to the conclusion that the *to chreōn* of the Anaximander fragment contains the first word of Being.[20]

Heidegger cuts the direct quotation from Anaximander down to a brief twelve words, dismissing even the traditionally accepted final *kata tēn tou chronou taxin* (according to the ordinance, order, or assessment of time) as not archaic enough—"too Aristotelian in tone and structure to be genuine."[21] I would nevertheless recall a similar image of the court or judgment (*dike*) of Time which appears in a fragment of a poem by Solon,[22] written nearly a generation before Anaximander. For this reason, I think it is possible to allow Anaximander's "*chronou taxis*" to stand. And indeed the evocation of the role played by time as the agent whose assessment reveals order is perfectly in keeping with Heidegger's own interpretation of *to chreōn* as "usage" rather than "necessity," since usage is usage only if revealed as such through time. With the "*chronou taxis*" retained as integral to the fragment, it is even possible to reconcile the seeming disparity between Heidegger's interpretation of *to chreōn* as "usage" and the more traditional translation that reads *to chreōn* as "necessity" or "what needs must be."

The word for time in the fragment is *chronos*, a period of time;[23] a time with before, during, and after; a time that, like the human life span, is essentially rectilinear. This sequential order is the *taxis* of *chronos*, and it is an assessment insofar as it reveals the cyclical order, the ebb and flow of *onta*, discussed earlier. The *taxis* of *chronos* reveals custom *as* necessity insofar as sequential time necessarily makes its assessment of events as repeated or not repeated, as customary or not, as cyclical or not. Only human rectilinear time, by establishing what is beginning, middle, and end, can reveal the occurrence of a repeated beginning, a repeated middle, a repeated end. What is cyclical or repeated is necessary; what is unrepeated, or unrepeatable, is not. It is rectilinear *chronos* which, as the arbiter or assessor of such necessity, determines what is *eu kata kosmon* and what is not. *Chronos*, sequential time, is the judge—both of earthly *chreōn* and of heavenly *kosmoi*, because it discloses the cyclical, regular movements of the celestial bodies. Reciprocally, the cycles of *kosmos* are what give *chronos* its measure: how many days (cycles of the sun), months (cycles of the moon), years (cycles of the seasons), etc. *Chronos* is the link that reveals both heavenly and earthly cycles as belonging to a single order, whose guide is some other boundless nature.[24]

To recapitulate what has emerged from this reading of Anaximander B1. The structure of Anaximander's universe is not yet hierarchical. He does indeed postulate a *hetera tis physis apeiros*, some other boundless nature-as-coming-to-be, which encompasses and, like the helmsman of a ship, steers (*kubernei*)[25] all things, giving rise to the heavens and the *kosmoi* within them. But this boundless source is *hetera*, "other": it is unknown and unnamable. It is not, as the later commentators name it, *to apeiron*, *the* Boundless. Although qualified as divine, it is also itself a quality, and as such a feature of experience,[26] discovered through experience.

This other boundless nature is the source of the **kosmoi** within the heavens, which in turn are the **genesis** for **onta** as the ebb and flow of hot, cold, moist, and dry dying into one another. This ebb and flow occurs according to usage, made recognizable as orderly or necessary by the assessment of time. As Anaximander speaks of it, the relationship between the **kosmoi** within the heavens and necessary usage would appear to be reciprocal, with **chronou taxis**, the order of rectilinear time, as the interpretive link between the two. The whole is an articulation of order in which the logic, far from being Aristotelian, is still very much rooted in what Jean-Pierre Vernant would call a "logic of ambiguity":[27] the logic of compact, mythical experience articulated in terms that are at once the **genesis** for the differentiations of an entire Western tradition.

——————— Anaximander's Image of **Kosmos** ———————

The B1 fragment, as well as other sources, attest that Anaximander spoke of order. And inasmuch as he *spoke* (rather than sang, as did the poets) of order, he was the first Greek writer of prose, which is to say that he wrote in the language of everyday speech.[28] In other words, his medium, to paraphrase Heraclitus, involved the transcription of a common or shared **logos**.[29] Common or shared speech (everyday language), transcribed, is prose.

Anaximander not only spoke of order, he also, it would appear, built order: a model, about which very little is known, but whose several parts seem to have included a celestial sphere, a map of the world, and a **gnōmōn**.

*Anaximander . . . was the first to discover a **gnōmōn**, and he set one up on the sundials[30] in Sparta . . . to mark solstices and equinoxes; and he also constructed hour-indicators. He was the first to draw an outline [**perimetron**] of earth and sea, but also constructed a [celestial] globe [**sphairan**].*[31]

Now it is possible to do as most commentators do and consider these three artifacts separately, each as evidence of Anaximander's proto-scientific activity: respectively proto-astronomical, proto-geographical, and proto-chronometrical. But, as I have attempted to demonstrate, the experience of order articulated in Anaximander B1 is still essentially compact, and so, I would contend, is the single order manifested through his allegedly disparate scientific activities. Anaximander's model of several parts was, intentionally, a single undertaking.

Although Anaximander B1 consists of only a few words that can be ascribed to Anaximander himself, this brief citation appears to have been part of a considerable body of written work, for as the tenth-century lexicographer Suda writes, Anaximander

*first discovered the equinox and solstices and hour-indicators, and that the earth lies in the centre. He introduced the **gnōmōn** and in general made known an outline of geometry. He wrote* On Nature [**Peri physeōs**], *Circuit of the Earth* [**Gēs periodos**], *and* On the Fixed Stars [**Peri tōn aplanōn**], *and a* Celestial Globe [**Sphairan**— "sphere"] *and some other works.*[32]

Based on the assumption that in Miletus ca. 560 B.C. the notion of **physis** (nature, the lived world) was interchangeable with the notion of **genesis** (generation, emergence, being born),

W. A. Heidel[33] has made an illuminating case for all these supposedly separate works actually being one book. In other words, if *physis is genesis*, then cosmology (or "astronomy"), geography, and history (or "chronometry"), being all *peri physeōs*, are all about coming-to-be, and are therefore essentially the same.

A similar unity of intent can be argued for the parts of Anaximander's built work—his "model," as I have called it, even though its parts were built at different scales, and probably constructed at different times and in different places, as the foregoing citation from Diogenes Laertius implies.

Anaximander did not, it would appear, invent either the map, the *gnōmōn*, or the celestial sphere. The Babylonians, with whom the Ionians were in close contact, had long been active in astronomy, and there were Babylonian precedents for both the *gnōmōn* and the map of the world.[34] But the Babylonian ordering of the world was despotic and hierarchical, and indeed the cosmological ordering activity, as Jean-Pierre Vernant has noted,[35] was integral to the role of the king. On the other hand, as the foregoing exploration of Anaximander B1 suggests, the understanding that Anaximander articulates is of an order that emerges from a reciprocal, not a hierarchical, relationship between the heavenly and the human.[36]

Anaximander made an image of *kosmos*, whose constituent parts were a celestial sphere, a map of the world, and a sun clock (*gnōmōn*, "hour-indicators," equinoxes and solstices). The overall image, pieced together from the sources, was of a spherical heaven made up of circular bands for planets, fixed stars, the moon, and, at the outer limit, for the sun. The earth in the shape of a column drum[37] hung suspended at the center. This flat cyclindrical earth, with a diameter three times its depth, stayed at the center by virtue of symmetry and balance, its equidistance from the outer edge preventing its fall in any given direction.

Theōria

The image, as an image, for the first time presented **kosmos** as a spectacle, a **theōria**. That such an image put order on display, as it were, can be seen to underscore the view of Anaximander as presiding at the birth of theory. This is indeed so if one accepts the usual modern view which stresses the speculative, nonparticipatory side of **theōria**, and interpolates, by reading backward, an assumed evolution from theory-as-contemplation to theory-as-opposed-to-practice. But there is another dimension to the whole question, for, when theory was born, Anaximander was not just the presiding midwife. He was also the baby.

In the life of a collective consciousness, the movement from compactness to differentiation is comparable to the birth and growth of an individual human being, who leaves the compactness of life *in utero*, where child is mother and mother is child, to acquire an increasingly differentiated understanding of the world. In the absolute darkness of the womb the child can, at the most, have only four senses—taste, hearing, smell, and touch. Only at birth, with the first and most definitive separation, does the child acquire its fifth sense and begin to *see*.[38]

This seeing, and the separation it presupposes, can be taken as emblematic of the birth of theory, for recent etymologies have shown, apparently with some conclusiveness, that the primary and original meaning of **theōros** was that of spectator. This modern claim is based on the derivation of *theōros* from *théa* (seeing, spectacle), and *horaō* (I see). Furthermore, *theōroi* were ambassadors to sacred festivals who left (were separated from) their native city to attend festivities elsewhere, and the assumption has been that these ambassadors observed, but did not participate. But a closer look at the ancient sources[39] shows that many *theōroi* did in fact participate by offering sacrifices, and by taking part in the dances and games.

It also is worth recalling that, while *théa*, with the accent on the first vowel, means seeing or spectacle, *theá*, with the accent on the final vowel, means goddess.[40] Indeed the ancient etymologists, from Plutarch onward, usually supposed that the first part of the word *theōros* was *theos*,[41] and that a *theōros* was someone who performed service to, or had care for, a god.[42] Moreover, the ancient etymologies, so readily dismissed by modern linguists, were much closer to the ancient experience than we are. The "caring for a god" aspect of *theōria* is especially evident when ancient sources use the word *theōros* to refer to a person who goes to consult an oracle.[43] Etymology is, at best, only a guide, and it is possible to claim, as Hannelore Rausch does,[44] that there is room for both gods and seeing in *theōria*.

The child's first gaze is a gaze of wonder. In Homer, the verb *theaomai*, for which the noun *théa* (spectacle) is a cognate, means to gaze upon with wonder, to marvel at.[45] The verb *thaumazein* (to wonder at, marvel) and the noun *thauma* (a wonder, a marvel) are very closely related to *theaomai*, for in Homer it is almost invariably what is seen that is wondered at: it is the *eyes* that marvel.[46]

Generally speaking, Homeric eyes fill with wonder on one of two occasions: first, when the spectacle suggests an unseen divine presence, and second, when the sight beheld is of something particularly well made. These two instances are not unrelated.

Thus, in the *Iliad*, Priam marvels at Achilles "for he was like the gods to look upon,"[47] and in the *Odyssey*, when, in Book XXIV, Odysseus emerges from his bath where the goddess Athena has restored him and made him taller and mightier than before, "his dear son marvelled at him, seeing him in presence like unto the immortal Gods."[48] Athena's too is the hidden divine presence at which, unwittingly, Telemachus marvels when he wonders at "the walls of the house and the fair beams and cross-beams of fir and the pillars . . . [which] glow in [his] eyes as with the light of a blazing fire."[49] The well-built house glows with the hidden presence of a goddess.

A stock phrase that occurs repeatedly in both the *Iliad* and the *Odyssey* is **thauma idesthai**, "a wonder to behold." Now, absolutely without exception, every time Homer qualifies something as "a wonder to behold" the thing so qualified is a beautifully, or divinely, crafted piece of work. So, in the *Iliad*, is Hera's chariot, with its bronze wheels whose felloes are of imperishable gold, over which "tires of bronze are fitted, a wonder to behold."[50] "A wonder to behold" is Rhesus' armor "cunningly wrought with gold and silver,"[51] and Patroclus' armor,[52] and Hephaestus' autokinetic bronze tripods that propel themselves about on wheels.[53] **Thauma idesthai**, in the *Odyssey*, are the walls of the Phaeacian city,[54] and Aphrodite's gown,[55] and the purple webs the Naiads weave on "long looms of stone"[56] in a cave in Ithaca. In Hesiod's *Theogony*, Pandora's veil is "a wonder to behold," as is her gold crown, on which is "much curious work [**daidala polla**]," for Hephaestus, who made it, put on it most of the creatures "which the land and sea rear up . . . like living beings with voices."[57]

Although there are several secondhand reports of Anaximander's cosmology itself (reports taken to be based on his book or books), an almost total absence of sources makes it virtually impossible to affirm anything definitive about the celestial globe as a model, except that it existed[58] and that it was an image of the heavens.

Assuming its three-dimensional existence, one might conjecture that it was, at least in part, built of metal, since

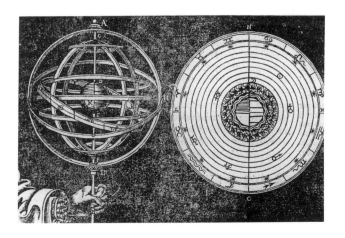

Vitruvius, De architectura libri decem,
translated and illustrated by Cesare Cesariano.
Cesariano's Latin caption reads
Mundi sphaerae coelestiu ac elementorum
quorum motus sic architectus est:
"The celestial sphere of the cosmos and its parts
which are set in motion as if by an architect."

curves, generally speaking, are easier to work in metal than in wood. Hammered bronze was a well-known medium in archaic Greece, where hammered bronze tripods, which had hemispherical basins, were highly valued. A hoplite's armor, where a proper fit was essential, was also of hammered bronze, and his helmet, a nearly spherical affair with nose and cheek pieces, was sometimes even hammered out of a single sheet of the metal.[59]

One might also conjecture that Anaximander's sphere was an assembly of several parts, since solar, lunar, stellar, and planetary rings figure largely in all reports of his cosmology.[60] These rings, like the felloes (*apsides*) of chariot wheels to which they were compared,[61] may, in the model, have been all metal, or may have been wood rimmed with bronze. The felloes of wooden wheels are quite complex to make, being constructed of several pieces of curved wood which must fit together exactly[62] in order to form the required circle. The rings, according to the sources, were supposed to have been hollow, and full of fire, with apertures or "breathing-holes" (*ekpnoas*) through which the fire showed to appear as the heavenly bodies.

However much, or little, of the reported cosmology appeared as literally represented in the model, it would have been a complex assembly requiring a careful adjustment of parts. The model may even, conceivably, have been mechanical,[63] with moving components, but even if its parts did not themselves move, much of the point of its construction would have been to reveal, by arresting them, the movements of the heavenly bodies.

When Vitruvius, whose sources as we know were Greek, speaks of the universe (*mundus*, which is how the Latins translated **kosmos**), his terms reflect those of the cosmology whose image first appeared in Anaximander's model.

*The universe is the entire compass of all nature and the configuration of the heaven with its stars. It rolls continually round the earth and sea, on the outermost pivots of its axis. For the innate power [at work] in these places is architectural, insofar as it has set up pivots to act as centres . . . and there around these pivots it has constructed the rims of wheels which the Greeks call **apsides** through which the heaven rolls eternally as on a lathe. In the midst thereof the earth and sea are naturally located in the central place.*[64]

Vitruvius', of course, is an architectural treatise and this passage appears at the beginning of his ninth book, which deals with *gnomonice*, the construction of clocks, the second of the three parts of architecture, which also includes building (*aedificatoria*) and machinery (*machinatio*).

The Map

It is with some hesitation that I use the word "map" to refer to Anaximander's image of the earth's surface. The ancient sources use the word **pinax**, which can mean tablet, chart, or simply plank, when they refer to the artifact itself, and **gēs periodos**, circuit of the earth, or way, path, or traveling (**hodos**) around the earth, when they refer to the geography. "Map" is rather too modern, but, unfortunately, discussion becomes very clumsy if its use is avoided. This said, there is slightly more information about Anaximander's "map" than there is about his sphere.

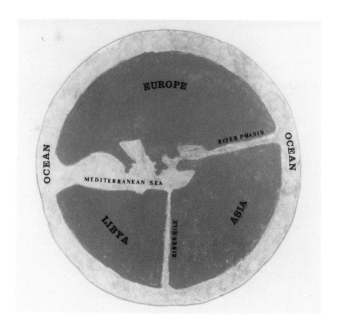

A reconstruction of Anaximander's map of the world.

Anaximander the Milesian, a disciple of Thales, first dared to draw the inhabited world on a tablet [**tēn oikoumenēn en pinaki grapsai**]; after him, Hecataeus the Milesian, a much-traveled man, made it more precise [**diēkribōsen**] so that it was a thing to be wondered at [**thaumasthēnai to pragma**]. . . . Now the ancients drew the inhabited earth as round, with Hellas in the middle and Delphi in the middle of Hellas, since it holds the navel [**ton omphalon echein**] of the earth.[65]

The earth, as noted, was cylindrical, "round like a **kionos lithos**," like a column drum, and "of its surfaces [**epipedōn**], one we walk on, and the other is on the opposite side."[66] To make his map, Anaximander would have, so to speak, sliced off the *oikoumenē*, the walked-upon surface, from the cylinder, for the map was indeed round, something Herodotus, in the fifth century, found a matter for ridicule:

*I laugh when I see that many have drawn circuits of the earth [**gēs periodous**] and none of them has explained the matter sensibly: they draw Okeanos running around the earth, which is round as if turned on a lathe [**eousan kukloterea hōs apo tornou**],*[67] *and they make Asia equal to Europe.*[68]

The column drums of the sixth-century Heraion in neighboring Samos, just across the bay from Miletus, were turned on a lathe,[69] and the proportion of their diameter to their thickness was roughly three to one, as it was for Anaximander's cylindrical earth.

Whether the tablet (*pinax*) on which the round *oikoumenē* appeared was itself round is difficult to determine. *Pinakoi*, in Homer, are platters on which food is served,[70] but they are also the planks of ships.[71] Herodotus tells of a *chalkeōs pinax*, a bronze map, that Aristagoras of Miletus brought to Sparta in 499–498 B.C., in order to persuade the Spartans to help in the Ionian revolt against the Persians. Aristagoras used the *pinax*, on which was cut (*enetetmēto*)[72] "the circuit of the entire earth the whole sea and all the rivers,"[73] to show Cleomenes, the Spartan king, the rich lands at the back of Ionia and also to locate Susa where, he said, the Spartans would find the great king's treasure.[74] Aristagoras' mission from Miletus took place about sixty years after Anaximander's *floruit*, and the only documented precedents for the *chalkeōs pinax* Herodotus speaks of are the maps of Anaximander and Hecataeus who, like Aristagoras, were both Milesians. Given the shortness of the tradition, it is unlikely that the *pinax* Aristagoras brought to Sparta would have been bronze had its predecessors been painted or drawn on wood. If so, the earlier maps too must have been bronze. It is even possible that the *pinax* Aristagoras brought to Sparta may have actually *been* one of the two known earlier *pinakoi*.[75]

To assume that Anaximander's *pinax* was bronze is not to assume that it was solid bronze. More probably, it would have been of composite construction, like the *hopla*, the great round shields, that were the salient, eponymous feature of a hoplite's armor. These were constructed out of wood, faced with bronze and emblazoned with cut-out insignia, or engraved.[76] It seems to me that Anaximander's map must have been very much like a shield, which is something that would account for a rather contentious phrase in one of the sources.

Hyppolytus says that the *schēma* (form, shape) of Anaximander's earth is "*guron*[77] [curved, like a hook, or with hunched shoulders], *stroggulon* [rounded], resembling a column drum." Kirk, Raven and Schofield take *guron* to refer to the circumference, or circular section, of the column drum, with *stroggulon* as a gloss on *guron*. Diels, however, read *guron* as convex, and took it to refer to the earth's surface.[78] The earth, in the ancient view, was at the center, with Hellas at the center of the earth and Delphi, with its *omphalos*, its convex navel-stone, at the center of Hellas. The earth was the *omphalos*, the convex boss or knob, at the center of the cosmos. Before Anaximander, Thales had claimed that the earth floated on the ocean, an image which recalls Calypso's "sea-girt isle" in the *Odyssey*: *omphalos thalassēs*, the navel of the sea.[79] Homeric shields are *omphaloessai*, bossed,[80] and the hoplite shields

Hoplites being piped into battle.
Painting on the proto-Corinthian Chigi olpe
at the Villa Giulia, Rome, ca. 640 B.C.

of Anaximander's own day were convex, with a flat rim running
around the outer edge.[81] Anaximander had Okeanos, the great
river of Ocean, running around the outer edge of his circular
map, as did that glorious forerunner of all cosmic maps,
Achilles' shield, as Homer describes it in the *Iliad*.[82] When
Hephaestus wrought Achilles' shield, "therein he wrought the
earth, therein the heavens, therein the sea."[83] Unlike Hephaestus, Anaximander made a separate model for the firmament,
but, I would suggest, the earth as a shield remained.

Anaximander made the first map. Hecataeus, a generation or so later, traveled widely and brought it to perfection,
or made it more precise (**diēkribōsen**). Hecataeus' travels were
a **theōria**, for Herodotus says of Solon, the great Athenian poet
and legislator, that "he, having made laws for the Athenians at

Battle between Hector and Achilles.

Black figure vase, late sixth century B.C.

their request, left his home for ten years and set out on a voyage to see the world,"[84] and the single Greek word, repeated again a few lines later, that is covered in the English translation by "to see the world" is *theōriēs*. Solon left Athens to "theorize," to be a *theōros*. Seen in the light of the foregoing discussion of *theōria*, Solon, as a traveler, was both a spectator and a servant of the gods. Seeing the world, for a Greek in the sixth century, meant viewing and wondering at the shifting surface of *physis/genesis* that shimmered in the Mediterranean light, an undertaking no doubt understood as comparable in nature to a sacred embassy (*theōria*) to Delphi or Olympia.

When Hecataeus brought Anaximander's map to perfection, he did not necessarily make a more exact representation, a more accurately scaled copy, of an earth viewed objectively

Anaximander and the Articulation of Order

on his travels. Whether on foot, under sail, or on horseback, the rigors of sixth-century B.C. travel would, one must imagine, have made a *theōria* of the kind undertaken by Solon or Hecataeus highly participatory. And never, in the terms the ancient sources actually used, was a map simply a representation of *gē*. What is today called a map, as has been noted, was spoken of as a *gēs periodos*, a circuit of, or journey[85] around, the earth, engraved or cut out *en pinaki*, on a tablet. The terms reveal mapmaking as an attempt to somehow arrest or make manifest the traveling itself; an effort to capture in an artifact the relationship between an earth still perceived as divine and alive and the human experience of journeying over her surface.

It is generally assumed that Hecataeus' perfection of Anaximander's map entailed the drawing of another, more accurate map, based on the earlier one which served as a model. However, if Anaximander's map was an assembly, constructed along the lines of a hoplite shield, with bronze plates fixed to a wooden backing, then the *diakribousa*, the perfecting, of the earlier map may very well have been just that: the removal of certain plates, the making of shinier, newer ones, and the more perfect adjustment of the entire assembly so that, as Agathemerus attests, "it became a thing to be wondered at."[86]

When Aristagoras went to Sparta to persuade Cleomenes to help the Ionians win their freedom, his tactic was an appeal to Cleomenes' greed. The lands at the back of Ionia were rich, and further east the Spartans would find the treasure of the great king. Aristagoras brought along a *chalkeōs pinax* to make his point, and as long as the map sustained his plea, Cleomenes was convinced. The map convinced him not, I would say, because it gave accurate directions for getting to the treasure, for two days later, when Aristagoras was forced to tell Cleomenes that Susa and its treasure were three months' journey distant (something the map had failed to reveal), Cleomenes lost his temper and dismissed Aristagoras summarily. Cleomenes was at first convinced because the map was *thauma idesthai*, "a wonder to behold," to use Homer's phrase, and because, as such, it made evident, by sharing their very identity, the splendor of oriental lands and their amazing wealth.

The Temporal Component: The **Gnōmōn**

For all that the **chalkeōs pinax** Aristagoras brought to Sparta was, as a **gēs periodos**, an image of traveling, it failed to reveal to Cleomenes how long it would take the Spartans to get to Susa. The map did not, could not, reproduce time. Besides the celestial globe and the map, Anaximander's model, his image of **kosmos**, needed yet another component to be complete.

Earlier it was noted that, in Achilles' shield, Hephaestus wrought both the heavens and the earth, whereas Anaximander's shield, if his **pinax** was indeed a shield, carried only an image of the **oikoumenē**, the inhabited earth, with the heavens accounted for in a separate model. Achilles' shield is almost entirely a temporal construction,[87] since, except for the bounding ocean around its edge, there is no way of actually locating any of the many narratives Homer says Hephaestus wrought into the shield's five-layered surface. The shield is an image of compact mythical experience. In it, the bounding ocean, the circular horizon of human experience, encompasses heaven and earth in time. There is nothing outside the shield.

Although Anaximander's, intentionally, was still a single artifact, it needed three parts for Homer's one. Anaximander's experience may, as yet, have been undifferentiated, and his intention, still, may have been to articulate that experience *as* undifferentiated, but what was noted earlier in discussing Anaximander B1—that the articulation was in terms that were the **genesis** for the differentiations of an entire Western tradition—also holds true for the parts of his cosmic model.

The third part of Anaximander's model was a sun clock. This, as we saw, was most probably not his own invention,

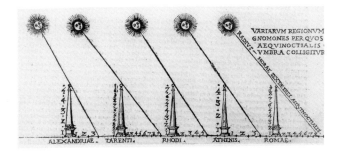

*"The different places where the
equinoctial shadows of gnomons are reckoned."*

even though Diogenes Laertius claims that it was,[88] for Herodotus says that "the Greeks learned from the Babylonians the **polos**[89] and the **gnōmōn** and the twelve parts of the day." Nevertheless, Anaximander did, it would appear, introduce the **gnōmōn** to Greece.

Now, a **gnōmōn**, in this particular context, is the pin or pointer set up **pros orthas**, at right angles,[90] on a sun clock, a vertical whose shadow indicates the sun's direction and height. A *gnōmōn*, however, is also a set square, or any vertical rod, and the suggestion seems to be that the generic feature of what the Greeks called a *gnōmōn* was orthogonality: the correct relationship between vertical and horizontal.

But the word *gnōmōn* derives from the verb *gignoscō* (I know), and the textual evidence indicates that, while the Greeks used it to speak of uprights, they also used it to speak of people: of the person who knows, the one who discerns. The noun *gnōmōn* does not appear in Homer, but the verb *gnoscō* does, and in almost all cases the knowing so referred to is knowing in the sense of the ability to recognize and interpret certain signs. Thus, for example, in Book VII of the *Iliad*, lots are cast and "Aias held forth his hand, and the herald . . . laid the lot therein; and Aias knew [*gnō*] at a glance the token on the lot."[91] Aias alone of the Achaean warriors recognized and was able to interpret the significance of the lot marked with his sign. Similarly, in the *Odyssey*, Halitherses is said to have "surpassed all men of his day in knowledge of birds [*ornithas gnōnai*] and uttering words of fate."[92] Birds, of course, are omens,[93] and the person who knows birds recognizes birds *as* omens. To know birds is to know which are omens (not all birds are) and, when they are, to be able to tell others what their significance is. The knower in both these examples is a mediator of signs, and Homeric usage clearly suggests that to know as *gnōnai* is different from knowing as *eidenai* (having seen) or knowing as *epistethai* (having skill).

A single passage in the *Odyssey* uses all three verbs for knowing, and differentiates their meanings quite well: "Then Odysseus of the many wiles answered her [Athena] and said: 'Hard is it goddess, for a mortal man to know [*gnōnai*, recognize, interpret] thee when he meets thee, how knowing [*epistamenōi*, having skill] so ever he be, for thou takest what shape whou wilt. But this I know well [*eu oida*, I *saw* well, have certain knowledge], that of old thou wast kindly to me.'"[94] In Greek, the aorist tense of the verb *horaō* (I see) is *oida* (I saw), and means "I know." What is known for certain is something that has been seen: *eidos*.[95]

The word *gnōmōn* as knowing thing, whether person or set square, is post-Homeric. In Aeschylus' *Agamemnon*, a *gnōmōn* is a person, an interpreter of *thesphatoi*,[96] of divine utterances or prophecies, which is to say a human link between heaven and earth. It is difficult, and perhaps not even very important, to establish which usage, person or set square, came first. Theognis uses *gnōmōn* to refer to a set square, or carpenter's square, in the mid-sixth century B.C., and Aeschylus uses it for interpreter at the beginning of the fifth. Whether a sundial pin was called a *gnōmōn* when it was first introduced to Greece is impossible to establish, since the Herodotus citation dates from the late fifth century, over a century after Anaximander. However, if uprightness had been the sole critical feature of sundial pointers or set squares, they would probably have been called something other than *gnōmōn*: *to orthon*, a straight-up thing, might, for example, have been a conceivable alternative. But the early Greek understanding was that uprightness, the relationship of vertical to horizontal, which is the relationship of the human body to the earth, had to do with knowledge as the recognition and interpretation of signs. As Vitruvius notes, people walk "not with head down, but upright," and it is the orthogonality of human posture that makes the human person the link between heaven and earth, that places him in the unique position of being able to "look upon the magnificence of the world and of the stars."[97]

With the sundial, the significance of the *gnōmōn* as the upright mediator of knowledge through interpretation becomes very explicit. If the sun's position at the equinoxes and solstices is to be accurately marked on the sundial's pavement, the pin must be set up at exactly 90 degrees to the ground, and the ground must be level. Theognis said that "the man who is *theōros*,[98] to whom the Delphic oracle *gives signs* [*sēmēnēi*][99] . . . must be more exact than the compass [*tornos*], the carpenter's rule [*stathmē*] and the *gnōmōn*, for if he adds one word, there is no hope to undo the evil, and if he subtracts one how would he not be guilty before the gods?"[100] The *gnōmōn* Theognis refers to is a set square, a carpenter's tool like the compass and ruler, and the context in which it is evoked makes it, like the other tools, an emblem of the exactitude required for proper interpretation of signs emitted from a divine source. The case of the *gnōmōn* of a sundial is comparable.

The construction of a sundial depended on knowledge of the movements of the heavenly bodies, which Anaximander revealed when he arrested them in the construction of his celestial globe. Knowledge of equinoxes and solstices established the fixed references needed to give journeying around the earth, *gēs periodos*, an image in a map.[101] Anaximander's earth was a disk, and its form did not reflect the spherical form established by heavenly *kosmoi*.[102] How then, in the archaic formulation, could the spherical heaven and cylindrical earth, so utterly different in configuration, relate to one another? The link that allowed for a reciprocal relationship between heavenly *kosmoi* and earthly *chreōn* (necessity or custom) was established, as I read Anaximander B1, *kata tēn tou chronou taxin*, according to the order of sequential time. In the third part of Anaximander's cosmic model, the link between spherical

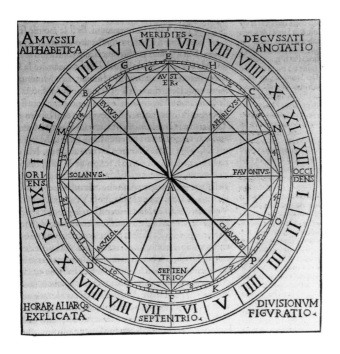

The gnomon here is at the center of a figure
which indicates the hours of the day and night
as well as the eight principal winds
and the division of the sky into sixteen parts.

*Anaximander's Image of **Kosmos***

heaven and flat earth is the mediating *gnōmōn* that obstructs the sun's light in order to throw a shadow which moved over a paved piece of earth in a graphic projection of celestial movement. The pavement, or analemma, was marked with equinoxes, solstices, and hour indicators, whose positions as reference points the *gnōmōn*, a human artifact set up at right angles to the earth, had also determined.[103] There may have been *durée*, lived time, before the *gnōmōn*, but before the *gnōmōn* there was no recognition or proper reading of celestial signs, and time, because it was not yet interpreted, had as yet no image: was not known in the sense of *eidenai*, to have seen. It was this human artifact, a concrete reflection both of human posture and of *chronos* as the rectilinear movement of time in the human life span, that revealed the heavenly *kosmoi* as cyclical and temporal. It was because of the *gnōmōn*, the mediating upright, that Plato was able to assert in the *Timaeus*, nearly 200 years after the *gnōmōn*'s introduction to Greece, that "Time [*chronos*] came into existence along with the Heaven [*ouranos*]," and that God created the sun, the moon, and the planets "for the determining and preserving of the numbers of Time."[104] Until the advent of the *gnōmōn* there could be no image, no *eidos*, of these numbers.

III

Daedalus
and the
Discovery of Order

Heaven, Plato has Timaeus say, was created in, or with, time "after the pattern of the Eternal Nature [*kata paradeigma tēs diaiōnias physeōs*]."[1] In Plato's *Timaeus*, the entire universe is an artifact constructed according to a *paradeigma* by a craftsman, a *dēmiourgos*. Unlike Anaximander's, Plato's universe would appear to be hierarchical. Anaximander's *hetera tis physis apeiros*, his unnamable, indefinite (*tis*, some), other boundless nature that encompasses and guides all things, seems to have become, in Plato, *the* (*tēs*)[2] definite, eternal nature, whose pattern, or *paradeigma* (which is what the Greeks called the architectural specimen[3] that a builder copied or used as a standard), is the immutable Idea that Plato's *dēmiourgos* copied when he made the world of Becoming in time.

One might assert that Plato's notion of the heavenly craftsman and his eternal *paradeigma* was "nothing but" the projection of the known, human way of building onto the unknown, divine or cosmic sphere. However, the question of pattern is somewhat more complex.

How, for instance, did the human builder's *paradeigma* become a *paradeigma*? Itself being made in time, it certainly did not exist eternally. But what, then, were the criteria which made *it*, and not some other specimen, the one to be copied? The answer it not simple.

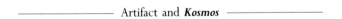

Artifact and *Kosmos*

The discovery of a pattern seems to me to be an inherent feature of the human experience of making. Whether he or she thinks about it or not, or is even aware of it, a person who makes something implicitly assumes the existence of an order or standard of rightness that transcends all recipes and rules of composition: a standard, a pattern, or—to use the Greek word—a *paradeigma* which both measures the work and is measured by it. This pattern can be thought of as a single, immutable template to be traced or copied, which appears to be how Plato understood it, or it can be thought of as a mutable rhythm governing a pattern of movement, like the figure of a dance: a rhythm or order (*kosmos*) that is rediscovered with each new tracing of the figure. Artists—and by "artists" I mean all people who make things: not just novelists, poets, composers, and painters, but also cooks, gardeners, and seamstresses, insofar as they are not assembly line workers—are an infinitesimal and powerless minority in the population of the modern Western world, but this was not always the case. The civilization of archaic Greece, which is to say Western civilization at its very roots, has been called a civilization of the artisan.[4] Contempt for artisans, such as the scorn latent in Socrates' derisive references to his alleged ancestor, was a later development. Indeed the Greeks themselves considered contempt for manual work to be foreign in origin, and not endemically Greek at all.[5]

It is my contention that, with the dawn of Greek thought, the pattern discovered, or allowed to appear, through making[6] was universalized to become the pattern that eventually came to be understood as the one embodied in the cosmos as we understand the word.

Homeric usage of *kosmos*, as discussed earlier, suggested an unnamed standard by which things were well (*eu*) according to, or not (*ou*) according to, order. Thersites' "measureless speech" in Book II of the *Iliad* is, like his misshapen body, disorderly, *ou kata kosmon*.[7] When Achilles slays a sheep to cook for his guest, Priam, in Book XXIV, "his comrades flayed it and made it ready well and duly [*eu kata kosmon*], and sliced it cunningly and spitted the morsels and roasted them carefully."[8] It is the speaking that reveals the absence of *kosmos* in the first instance and the preparation of food that reveals its presence in the second: it is through *making* that *kosmos* appears, or does not. In fact *kosmos*, at times, seems to share the very identity of making. After Odysseus has applauded the minstrel Demodocus in Book VIII of the *Odyssey*, saying "above all mortal men do I praise you . . . for *liēn* [exceedingly] *kata kosmon* do you sing of the fate of the Achaeans," he then goes on to ask the bard to change his theme and "sing the building [*kosmon*] of the horse of wood."[9] The *kosmon* of the Trojan horse, translated by A. T. Murray, the Loeb translator, as its building, is taken in this context as the neuter present participle of the verb *kosmeō* (arrange, order, adorn). However, the line could also, with perfect grammatical correctness, have been translated as "sing the *order* of the horse of wood," with *kosmon* understood as the accusative of the masculine noun *kosmos*. There was, it must be remembered, no grammar[10] in the Greece of the eighth century B.C. when the Homeric epics were transcribed. It was only much later that *kosmon* as the act of arran*ging* was distinguished, grammatically, from *kosmon* as the fact of arrange*ment*.[11] The same argument makes it possible to read the phrase *kata kosmon* both as "according to arran*ging*" and as "according to order, or arrange*ment*."

Kosmos can also be read as adornment, especially feminine, for indeed "cosmetic" comes from *kosmos*. *Chrōs* (skin or color) is the Homeric word for the living body, which was understood as a surface[12] and the bearer of visibility, visibility being the guarantor of existence or being. For the Greeks appearing was surface, with *epiphaneia* a word used for both. For them, when a woman *kosmēse* (adorned) herself, she wrapped her *chrōs* in a second skin or body, in order to bring the living surface-body so clothed to light; to make it appear. If women, in ancient Greece, were essentially invisible, cosmetic *kosmos* made them visible.[13] In archaic statuary, ideal youths (*kouroi*) stride forward, one foot resolutely planted before the other. They are always naked. Ideal maidens (*korai*) stand stock still, feet together, beautifully dressed.

In the *Iliad*, when Hera sets out to seduce her husband Zeus,[14] she washes and perfumes herself, and plaits her hair, and clothes herself in a robe wrought for her by Athena with cunning skill (*daidala polla*), fastening it with gold brooches, and belting it with a girdle with a hundred tassles. In her pierced ears she hangs earrings "with three clustering drops," under her feet binds fair sandals, and over all drapes a "glistening veil, white as the sun." And when, with the donning of these wonderfully crafted artifacts, she had, according to Homer, *thekato*, made or set up, *kosmos* all about her body (*panta peri chroi . . . kosmon*),[15] she went to ask Aphrodite to give her love and desire, in order to accomplish her mission of persuading Zeus to side with the Achaeans against the Trojans.

Similarly, in the Homeric hymn to Artemis, when the goddess goes to Delphi to order (*artyneousa*) the lovely dance (*choros*) of the Muses and Graces, she "hangs up her curved bow and her arrows," there to command (*hēgetai*), gracefully leading the dances, having *kosmos* about her body (*peri chroi kosmon echousa*).[16] Here especially, but also in other passages where female divinities adorn themselves, or, as Homeric language actually describes it, wrap themselves in *kosmos*, in order to go dancing, the suggestion is that the ordering of the dance

Korē dedicated by Cheramyes at the temple of Hera at Samos,
ca. 560 B.C.

is a reflection of their adornment, or ordered second skin, and
vice versa. As *kosmos* clothes the body to make it appear, so,
through the dance, *kosmos* clothes the ground to make it
appear, even as, in the Homeric hymn to Selene, the radiance
of the moon (of all the heavenly bodies surely the most feminine) "is shown from heaven to dance around—or clothe
[*elissetai*]—the earth, and much *kosmos* arises from her shining
light."[17]

    Kosmos, in Homer but especially after him, is also polit-
ical or moral order,[18] and it is this order, the order of the

newly emerged *polis*, that Jean-Pierre Vernant has claimed the Ionians, beginning with Anaximander, made spatial and geometric and projected onto the universe.[19] However, the recognition of *kosmos* already, as I have argued, assumed a standard of rightness external to itself. As will be discussed more fully in due course, the city was made, and continually remade, in a making that was itself a discovery of *kosmos*. The order of the *polis* was not immanent and then projected as transcendent, as Vernant's argument implies. Rather, I would say, the making of the city implicitly assumed a transcendent order from the very outset.

The city was an artifact, and the *dēmiourgos*, at least in the early stages of emerging Greek consciousness, was as much the legislator who made public order as the craftsman who made the *kosmos* of things. Indeed, as we shall see, craftsman and legislator were generically the same.

Thus, the public or political order, which Vernant understands as having been launched into the heavens with Anaximander and the dawn of Western thought, is part of a more general order of making, or making appear, of which the *kosmos* of the *polis* is only one aspect. The circular seating of elders in assembly (the very embodiment of political *kosmos*) is but one of several ways in which order may become manifest. As the thirteenth Homeric epigram puts it:

*Children are a man's crown, towers of a city; horses are the **kosmos** of a plain, and ships the **kosmos** of the sea; wealth will make a house great, and reverend princes [**basileis**] seated in assembly [**ein agorēi**] are **kosmos** for folk to see.*

If I have been rather insistent in my speculations about the physical existence of Anaximander's cosmic model as a three-part artifact, it is because the very roots of his cosmology, which to my mind is inseparable from the thinking expressed in the fragment, can be seen to lie in the actual making, in the *kosmon* (arrang*ing*/arrange*ment*), of that model. Granting that the model was indeed made, and that its making was the generation, the *genesis*, of what is expressed verbally in the speculation, the implication is not that the form the model took was then projected onto the heavens. Rather, I would insist, the order of the heavens was simultaneously made to appear and *discovered through* the making. The details of the model's construction may have been as I have imagined them— or they may not. This is basically irrelevant.

Anaximander's cosmic model, as he himself was well aware, could have taken any number of forms, for as he speaks of them, the heavens and the *kosmoi* within them are plural.[20] Indeed, part of his speculation was the positing of the existence of unlimited worlds.

His model, once made, was recognized as having coherence, and confirmed the configuration of a universe known from experience to have the Earth, and Hellas, at its center. Because of this, and because there were no others, Anaximander's became *the* model: in Plato, the *paradeigma* for a *dēmiourgos* whose creation of *kosmos* was no longer a question of making a world appear, but a matter of representing one through the duplication of an immutable pattern.

F. M. Cornford and Jean-Pierre Vernant, among others, have argued that much of the mythical world still clings to Anaximander's speculation. Although my emphasis diverges somewhat from theirs, this view has been assumed in the present discussion, where it is suggested that the compactness of mythical experience continues to be the ground for the differentiated expressions of Anaximander's work. And this, I claim, holds true both for the speculation and for his built work, whose sense the B1 fragment articulates in prose.

The built work (apart from its theory)[21] further reflects a mythical understanding, for this cosmic model, while acting as the ***paradeigma*** for all subsequent cosmologies until the time of Galileo, was also a ***daidalon***, which shared most, if not all, of the essential features attributed to the creations of the legendary Daedalus.

Cutting, Assembly, ***Harmonia***

Françoise Frontisi-Ducroux concludes,[22] after a detailed study of Homeric usages, that the word ***daidalon***, in its most limited and primitive applications,[23] denoted a cutting up or cutting out (*découpage*), either in wood or in metal, and this *découpage* was invariably associated with the complementary notion of adjustment, or fitting together. Armor, notably that of Achilles, whose bronze, gold, and silver shield was wrought in five layers by the divine smith Hephaestus, was particularly ***daidalon***, for indeed armor was an assembly of cut-out pieces. Works of carpentry, especially ships, were also ***daidala***.

It is significant that ***hylē***, the "matter" later set up in opposition to the intelligent formative principle in the Aristotelian form-and-matter differentiation,[24] was first, in Homeric usage and even later, forest or woodland, or, more specifically, wood or timber.[25] When Odysseus the *tecton*, the boat builder, builds his boat in Book V of the *Odyssey*, assisted by the nymph Calypso (who, incidentally, has dressed very carefully for the occasion),[26] the timber he cuts and fits together would originally have been *hylē*.

*Twenty trees in all did he fell, and trimmed them with the axe; then he cunningly [**epistamenōs**] smoothed them all and made them straight to the line [**epi stathmēn**]. Meanwhile Calypso, the beautiful goddess, brought him augers; and he bored all the pieces and fitted them to one another [**harmoniēsin arēren**], and with pegs and morticings did he hammer it together.[27]*

Archaeological evidence about how ancient boats were actually put together strongly suggests that when Odysseus built his boat, he built it in the image of the Homeric body, of *chrōs* as living surface: *epiphaneia*, appearing.[28]

There are, says Lionel Casson,

basically, two ways of putting together a wooden hull. One is to set up a skeleton of keel and frames (ribs) and fasten a skin of planks to it. The other dispenses with the skeleton and simply builds up a shell of planks, pinning each plank in some fashion to its neighbors.[29]

The ancient Greeks, and Odysseus, used the latter method, carefully fastening plank to plank with painstakingly crafted mortise-and-tenon joints. With little apparent concern for speed or ease of construction, Odysseus shaped his boat from

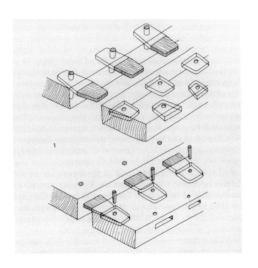

Joining the planks of ships by means of mortises and tenons.

the outside in, as a shell or watertight skin. Only afterward, if the shell so constructed appeared to need additional reinforcement, would he have added an internal structure. "The Greco-Roman shipwright," continues Casson,

carried out the joinery with such care that it more resembles cabinet work than carpentry. . . . The work involved was laborious, but the reward was a hull of remarkable strength at a great saving in weight and bulk.

Sooner or later he was bound to realize that he did not have to go through the time-consuming process of mortising and tenoning the planks together, to realize that, if he used heavier frames he could put these up first, quickly and easily fasten the planking directly to them, and end up with a hull which, though less strong, was perfectly adequate. [30]

Hylē, one might say, was the stuff of Odysseus' boat. If, in search of evolutionary causes, one reads backward from the later understanding of *hylē* as brute matter,[31] it is deceptively simple to claim that the preclassical understanding of *hylē* as forests and timber was that these were "nothing but" the unformed matter of boats, or that *hylē* as firewood[32] was "nothing but" the fuel that feeds the flame. This would be very misleading. In preclassical Greece, *hylē*, as forest, timber, or firewood, was part of a divine and deathless *physis*. *Hylē*, wood, was cut up, probably with all the circumspection devoted to the cutting up of a sacrificial victim, to be remade, in order that it might reappear in another guise—as a boat or, even more magically, as flame—even as reassembling the bones of a cut up, sacred, sacrificial animal under its flayed skin made the animal magically "reappear."[33]

The adjective *arērōs*, meaning well-adjusted or perfectly fitted together, is, apparently, a very old word whose use is traceable as far back as the Mycenaean Linear B script.[34] In *arērōs* is both the etymological and experiential root of the whole notion of *harmonia*, in Homer a ship-building term with special reference to the joints.[35] Only later, in the classical period, does it become the notion that would be forged, link by link, into the Great Chain of Being,[36] one of the most persistent images of cosmic harmony in the whole history of Western culture.

Anaximander's model, like Odysseus' boat, must, as I have imagined it, have been *arērōs*, in the oldest sense of the term. Although it was meant, specifically, to be a cosmic model, and although it did indeed, for the first time, reveal a clear notion of fixed proportions,[37] it was, I would suggest, primarily because as a model it was *arērōs* that Anaximander's construction was able to reveal all that other unseen harmony. It is important to recall that the **hetera tis physis apeiros** of Anaximander B1, the "some other boundless nature" that is the source of the heavens and the **kosmoi** within them, is thought of in navigational terms as steering, guiding, or acting as helmsman for (**kubernein**) all things.

In the wave of enthusiasm for the unseen harmony disclosed, as I believe, through the model (Pythagoras followed hard upon Anaximander), the role the model played was forgotten by Western thinkers, to the point where today some philosophical historians even doubt that the celestial sphere, the first of its three parts, ever existed.[38]

Vitruvius, thanks no doubt to his Greek sources, still understood the cosmic role of artifacts perfectly. Speaking of the nature of the winds, he says,

Wind is a wave of air moving hither and thither indefinitely. It comes to be [nascitur] *when heat meets moisture, the rush of heat generating a mighty current of air. . . . That this is true is made very clear by bronze aeolipyles which* [*show how*] *the truth of divinity* [divinitatis veritatem] *is unveiled by the artful inventions of things* [artificiosis rerum inventionibus] *which reveal the hidden orders of the sky* [latentibus caeli rationibus].[39]

Vitruvius also knew that it is only *after* it has been made, when the artifice has become a **theōria**, a spectacle, that the clever invention can reveal the divine cosmic order. After describing the action of aeolipyles, he continues, "Thus it is possible to know and judge [scire et iudicare] from a small and very short spectacle [parvo brevissimoque spectaculo] the great and vast order of the sky and of the nature of the winds."[40]

Aeolipilarum figura.

Weaving

In the *Odyssey*, generally held to be of later composition and/
or transcription than the *Iliad*,[41] the notion of things that are
daidala—"cunningly crafted" and "curiously wrought" are two
common translations of the word—comes to apply more and
more frequently to textiles. In Hesiod this usage becomes
virtually exclusive, with the gold crown of Pandora referred
to earlier[42] a notable exception. Textiles that are *daidala* are
so qualified when they are tightly woven—*arērōs*, like a ship's
joints—and have a luminous sheen. Like the metal plates of a
warrior's armor, they shimmer with dancing light and seem to
have a life of their own, as do those other *daidala*, the *xoana*,
or wooden cult statues, evoked at the very beginning of this
essay.

Textile *daidala* are often described as *poikilon*, which most translators render as "embroidered." However, Frontisi-Ducroux argues very convincingly[43] that the iridescent colored patterns which made a cloth *poikilon*[44] (and *daidalon*) were not embroidered, or applied over a preexisting surface, but were actually woven into the surface of the fabric itself. If so, the pattern would have appeared *with* the surface of the cloth, whose making would have been an activity that entailed great skill and a highly complex pattern of movement of shuttle over loom. The word for weaving, or plying the loom, is *hyphainein*, which literally means to bring to light,[45] or make visible, and the word for surface, as noted earlier, is *epiphaneia*.

Pherecydes of Syros,[46] the mythographer and theogonist active around the middle of the sixth century B.C. and thought to have postdated Anaximander, wrote, like Anaximander, in prose. In his myth of the wedding of Zas and Chthonie, Zas, as a wedding gift, clothes Chthonie with "a great fair cloth" on which (or *in* which—*en autōi*) he *poikillei Gē*, the Earth.[47] It is the woven cloth, or perhaps its very weaving, that makes Earth, with all its variegated, scintillating patterns, appear. Significantly, it is this mythical veiling of Chthonie, whereby Earth is made to appear, that the papyrus here cited claims as the first *anacalyptēria*, or *un*veiling, which was (and still remains) part of the traditional Greek wedding ceremony. The weaving of the cloth is an unveiling insofar as the person veiled (Earth, or the bride) only appears, properly speaking, after she has been clothed.

Surface and Appearing

The marvels Homer and Hesiod qualify as **thauma idesthai**, a wonder to behold, are each and every one of them **daidala**. The metalwork, carpentry, or weaving that bring them to light, so that they may be beheld, do so through **kosmon**, which is simultaneously arranging, ordering, and adorning. Craft gives things life, and it is no accident that **tiktein** is to give birth, **tektein** to build, and **technē** a letting appear.[48]

Live body (**chrōs**) and dead body (**soma**) were two different things for the preclassical Greeks—not a single entity, the one animated, the other not. The living human body, as **chrōs**, was both a skin or surface and an appearing (**epiphaneia**). The Christians, very much later, called the divine Child's appearing Epiphany, but in the early Greek understanding such would have been the appearing of any child—of any human being. This was not because the Greeks especially revered human life, in the modern sense: children were systematically exposed at birth if the father deemed them undesirable. Rather it was because of the early Greek perception of, and keen sensitivity to, what was actually given in experience.

The divinity of Greek gods and goddesses rested on the fact of their always appearing, and never entirely disappearing, for gods were divine not by virtue of their always having existed, since being born, **genesis**, was the essential feature of everything, including gods. Gods were divine because they were **athanatoi**, deathless. This unending appearingness of the Greek gods, their **genesis** which is life and movement, is what resided in the scintillating surface of the **daidalon**. Insofar as the appearing of the **daidalon** was understood as itself the product of reassembly, the **daidalon** must also have been understood as something that could always be remade. Like the gods, and unlike the human person (**brotos**, mortal), the **daidalon** never entirely disappeared. It is because it was itself a deathless appearing that the well-made, the cunningly crafted thing was able to reveal an unseen divine presence. Thus, for example, are the gold and silver dogs, crafted by Hephaestus, which guard Alcinous' palace in Book VII of the *Odyssey*, **athanatous ontas**, deathless beings, just like gods.[49]

The deathlessness of a god or goddess was not contingent upon changelessness. Rather, the facility for appearing and reappearing under different guises was one of the basic qualities of divinity. Indeed, Ovid retells the whole of Greco-Roman mythology in terms of such changes in his *Metamorphoses*. As Odysseus says to Athena in a passage cited earlier,[50] "Hard is it goddess, for a mortal man to know thee when he meets thee, . . . for thou takest what shape thou wilt." As already stressed, that a god or goddess might be known, or recognized, as elusive was one of the fundamental reasons for tying down Daedalean **xoana**.

Once a year the **xoanon** of the Samian Hera was unbound and hidden in a willow tree, where it was then rediscovered and brought back to its shrine in the temple.[51] Whatever it had to do, and it was probably much, with the cyclical course of the seasons, this ancient ritual would also have been a yearly revelation of appearing and reappearing as the very essence of all that is divine, **athanatos**. And lest the significance of the ritual eclipse the physical presence of the artifact, it should be remembered that it was through the statue's presence that divinity was revealed, and that without it the ritual could not even have taken place.

Choros and Labyrinth

When the legendary Daedalus[52] fled Athens, his birthplace, because he was being prosecuted for having murdered his nephew Talos out of jealousy for Talos' alleged invention of the compass, he went to Knossos in Crete, where he took up residence in the court of King Minos. There he built the celebrated mechanical cow in which Queen Pasiphae hid herself in order to seduce the bull for which she had developed a passion, and from their unnatural union was born the Minotaur, a man with the head and neck of a bull. Minos then had Daedalus build the Labyrinth in which to conceal the monstrous evidence of his wife's infidelity.

Every nine years seven Athenian youths (*kouroi*) and seven maidens (*korai*) were sent to Knossos as food for the Minotaur. When Theseus, son of the Athenian king Aegeus, was sent to Crete as one of their number, he fell in love with Ariadne, Minos' daughter, and slew the Minotaur, with Ariadne's thread guiding his way back to the entrance of the Labyrinth from the Minotaur's lair.

Daedalus then built a *choros*, a dancing floor, for Ariadne. Afterward, Theseus and Ariadne fled Knossos, and upon their arrival at the sacred island of Delos, the birthplace of Apollo, they danced a dance cryptically known as the "crane dance."

It is in the *choros*, considered together with the Labyrinth, and in the crane dance, which the legend places at about the midpoint of Daedalus' career, that the whole notion of making and remaking, of appearing and reappearing, becomes most transparent.

The earliest reference to Daedalus' *choros*, and the only reference to Daedalus in Homer, occurs at the end of the description of Achilles' shield in Book XVIII of the *Iliad*:

*Therein furthermore the famed god of the two strong arms cunningly wrought [**poikille**—wove] a dancing-floor [**choros**] like unto that which in wide Knossos Daedalus fashioned [**ēskēsen**]*[53] *of old for fairtressed Ariadne. There were youths dancing and maidens of the price of many cattle, holding their hands upon the wrists one of the other. Of these the maidens were clad in fine linen, while the youths wore well-woven tunics faintly glistening with oil; and the maidens had fair crowns, and the youths had daggers of gold hanging from silver baldrics. Now would they run round with cunning [**epistamenoisi**] feet exceeding lightly, as when a potter sits by his wheel that is fitted between his hands and makes trial of it whether it will run; and now again would they run in rows toward each other. And a great company stood around the lovely dance [**choros**], taking joy therein; and two tumblers whirled up and down through the midst of them as leaders in the dance.*[54]

One of the many things this passage reveals is that *choros* is not only dancing floor, or dancing place, but the dance itself.[55] The word *choros* (or one of its compounds) is used nine times in the *Iliad*, but only once, at the beginning of this passage where the reference is specifically to Daedalus' construction, does it appear, unequivocally, to mean a *place* for dancing, and not the dance.[56] Now, although these kinds of statistics can be seen as inconclusive at best, and at worst completely irrelevant, it is nevertheless to my mind significant that, in the later *Odyssey*, *choros* continues to refer to the dance, but appears several times as dancing floor. There is one notable passage where Odysseus is among the Phaeacians "famed for their ships,"[57] whose beautiful cities, palaces, gardens (described as *kosmētai*),[58] and harbors Homer extolls, and to whom, says their king Alcinous, the banquet, the lyre, and the dance (*choros*) are dear:[59]

*Then stood up the masters of the lists [**aisymnētai**], nine in all, men chosen from among the people [**dēmioi**], who in their gatherings were wont to order all things aright. They levelled a dancing-place [**choron**] and marked out a fair wide ring, and the herald came near, bearing the clear-toned lyre for Demodocus.*[60] *He then moved into their midst and around him stood boys in the first bloom of youth, well-skilled in the dance, and they smote the goodly dancing-floor [**choron theion**] with their feet.*[61]

Significantly, what Demodocus sings of, while the dancing is going on, are the inextricable bonds (**desmoi apeirones**)[62] which Hephaestus, the patron of craftsmen, forged to trap his wife Aphrodite and her lover, Ares, in the *flagrant délit* of their adulterous embraces.

Diodorus Siculus uses the same adjective, **apeiros**, to describe the tortuous dead-end passages of Daedalus' Labyrinth,[63] for **apeiros** means not only boundless but also, like **aporia**,[64] without escape, which is also to say unmeasured, or immeasurable. It is the measure of Ariadne's dance, the confused regularity of the "moving maze" traced by the passage of "well-taught feet,"[65] which spins the thread that leads out of the Labyrinth, and goes on to weave another. The preclassical Greeks could answer riddles, and interpret oracles, but they had no knowledge of problem solving. In the still-living imagery of Minoan murals, slim Cretan youths leap over the horns of death-dealing bulls in order to *dance* with them. For the early Greeks, the dangers of **aporia** were not problems to be solved but the basic precondition for artifice.

This fundamental understanding, which is what made the **epistēmē** of the archaic period knowledge-as-skill and the **sophia** of Daedalus skill in craft, is what made the crane dance or the Trojan game (both Labyrinth dances under different names), and indeed all forms of mazes, so pervasive throughout archaic Hellas especially in relation to the founding of cities.[66]

The Labyrinth, it is essential to realize, appears under two very different and seemingly self-contradictory guises. When we read about it in the ancient sources, the narratives always stress its complexity and confusion. The narrative accounts invariably speak of tortuous dead-end passages that are inescapable. Like the *desmoi apeirones* that Hephaestus fashions to trap his wife and her lover, or the *daidalos peplos* in whose endlessness (*en d'atermoni*)[67] Clytemnestra traps Agamemnon in order to stab him to death—the elaborately woven robe which the murderous queen calls an *apeiron amphiblēstron*, an inextricable net[68]—like these, the narrative Labyrinth is the terrifying embodiment of anarchic *aporia*.[69]

Yet the *image* of the Labyrinth, as it appears on Cretan coins as well as in all later representations from Roman mosaics to the floors of Gothic cathedrals and Renaissance gardens, is not confused at all. Whether circular or square, it invariably has a very clear and regular configuration. The image of the Labyrinth, its *eidos*—the thing seen and therefore known for certain—is the *choros*.[70]

The Western tradition has been to interpret the skillful embrace of *aporia* revealed through the construction of *choros* and Labyrinth as a question of imposing order on chaos. This is a misrepresentation whose roots may well lie with the Romans.[71] Certainly the Romans, those expert pavers of straight roads which for centuries sustained the march of the bearers of *pax Romana*, did not, like the early Greeks, trace paths through journeying. And it is Ovid who, in typical Roman fashion, latinizes Hesiod's coming-to-be of earth and sky[72] as

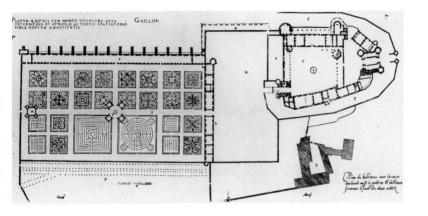

*Plan for the garden of Gaillon
with two labyrinths, one square, the other circular.*

the imposition of order on chaos. Ovid calls chaos a *rudis indigesta moles*, a crude, confused, and shapeless mass,[73] which, like the *hylē* of classical and postclassical Greek thought, is brute matter to be subdued and shaped.

This differs from Hesiodic **Chaos**, but how, exactly, is difficult to make precise, for Hesiod, to the despair of scholars, never actually says what **Chaos** *is*. He simply says that **Chaos** *genet'*, "**Chaos** came to be"—first, before "wide-bosomed earth."[74] Later in the *Theogony* he explicitly says that **Chaos** is the space between heaven and earth.[75] This, together with the fact that the word **chaos** appears to derive from the verb **chaskein**, yawn or gape, has led scholars to identify **chaos** with a primordial gap or chasm, similar to the *ginnunga-gap* of Nordic mythology.[76] There are other passages in the *Theogony* which seem to identify **Chaos** with the murky underworld regions of Tartarus,[77] giving it a dimension of obscurity and confusion which, on the most generic level, bears some resemblance to the chaos of Ovid's description. What is totally absent in Hesiod, however, is any suggestion that there is an opposition between *chaos* and *kosmos*, or order.[78] As Hesiod tells it, *Chaos*, simply, came to be first, necessarily, it would seem, as a precondition for the coming-to-be of heaven and earth. *Chaos* is certainly not the matter out of which heaven and earth are actually made, but neither is it, entirely, the featureless space into which they are born.

As is so often the case when one attempts to enter into the early Greek perception of things, the mistake to be avoided at all costs is an either/or kind of assessment: *chaos* is *either* a gap *or* a confused and shapeless mass. *Chaos* is both and neither. Confusion is a quality of early Greek *chaos* insofar as, until it is measured, *chaos* is immeasurable. But when earth and sky have come to be, *chaos* can become the space between them, because earth and sky have become its measure. Similarly, *chaos* under the guise of the human experience of *aporia* is a precondition for the coming-to-be of both Labyrinth and *choros*, which together are its embodiment and its measure.

It was noted earlier that the word *choros* tends, with the passage of time, increasingly to mean dancing place as well as dance. This reflects the tendency toward localization or spatialization of the purely temporal—just as when, with Anaximander's map, *gēs periodos* both localized Homeric journeying (*hodos*) and mitigated the temporality of Achilles' shield. What can be detected in this is an important reversal in the very process of emergence.

Before Daedalus made Ariadne's dancing floor in the *Iliad* (to extrapolate from the admittedly limited textual evidence), there was no thought given to the *place* for the dance. Dancing was dancing, and the measure of the dancing floor was the measure of the dance itself. The place appeared with the dance and disappeared when the dance was over. Its independent status was not even an issue. When *choros* first becomes dancing place, it does not cease to be dance, however. For in the passage cited, Homer says that on Achilles' shield Hephaestus *poikille* (wove) a dancing floor like the one Daedalus made for Ariadne, but he does not say that the dancing floor was made first and that only then did the dance take place. In fact, he says nothing about the dancing floor at all; the description is devoted entirely to the dance.[79] The dancing floor seems to emerge with the dancing of the youths and maidens, who, it should be noted, are very *kosmētai* in all their finery and with the pattern of their movement. Hephaestus' handiwork is described in terms of weaving, which both reflects the weaving of the dancer's feet and is reflected in the rhythms of the poet's verse. Without these, the dancing floor had, as yet, no surface and no appearing.

In the later passage cited from the *Odyssey*, Demodocus (and Homer) still sing while the young people dance. But this time, the sequence of the narrative clearly indicates that the "goodly dancing-floor" was leveled first.

Hesiod postdates both the Homeric epics, and I would speculate that Hesiod's enigmatic *Hē toi men prōtista Chaos genet'*, "at the very, very first[80] *Chaos* came to be," as the precondition for the coming-to-be of "wide-bosomed Earth," is a reflection of the same emerging awareness that begins to demand that the place for the dance be a precondition for dancing.

When Hephaestus makes Achilles' shield, the construction is a temporal one, but in the sequence of Homer's narrative there is no suggestion that the construction of one of the shield's features depends on the previous construction of some other feature. There are, for example, two cities on the shield, one at peace, the other at war. Homer speaks of the city at peace first, but there is no indication that the appearance of the city at war in some way depends on the previous appearance of the city at peace. Homer simply says that Hephaestus fashioned one and then the other. Whatever reason there may be for describing the city at peace first, it is not an evolutionary or teleological one. The shield is the cosmos, with Ariadne's dance, as the last feature described, a summation of its entire cosmic significance. Although the shield is temporal, in it there is as yet, to recall Anaximander's **chronou taxis**, no *order* of time.

In Hesiod's *Theogony*, however, the order of time is the very pole and axis of the entire narrative. **Chaos** came to be, and then Earth, who gave birth to sky and sea, and so on, in a genealogy that extends from the first Titans right down to Zeus. The recital of this genealogy, in which each birth is dependent upon the previous one in the sequence, has as its purpose the legitimation of Zeus and his reign of Justice. Hesiod is unequivocal in the revelation of his intentions. The order of the cosmos, which here is the just reign of Zeus, hangs upon the sequential order of **chronos**, the rectilinear time of the upright, mortal, human person.

Wings

But Daedalus, they say, on learning that Minos had made threats against him because he had fashioned the cow, became fearful of the anger of the king and departed from Crete.[81]

There are two versions of Daedalus' escape from Crete. Ovid's is the more familiar one.

Icarus and Daedalus (fragment).

Daedalus made two pairs of wings, fastening "feathers together with twine and wax at the middle and bottom; and, thus arranged, he bent them with a gentle curve, so that they looked like real birds' wings."[82] One pair was for himself, the other for his son Icarus, whom, before setting out, he cautioned thus:

I warn you, Icarus, to fly in a middle course, lest, if you go too low, the water may weight your wings; if you go too high, the fire may burn them. Fly between the two . . . fly where I shall lead [me duce carpe viam].[83]

The sequel is well known. Icarus did fly too high, the sun melted the wax that held his wings together, and he fell into the sea near Samos and was drowned.

Diodorus acknowledges that "certain writers of myths"[84] do indeed give this, as he seems to consider it, dubious account of the story, but he tells another, apparently to his mind more authentic one. Daedalus and his son, with Pasiphae's help, escaped in a boat. It is Icarus' recklessness in disembarking on an island near Samos, henceforth called Icaria, that causes his death, and Daedalus then sails on to Sicily.

Pausanias speaks of *two* boats:

For when he [Daedalus] was fleeing from Crete in small vessels which he had made for himself and his son Icarus, he devised for the ships sails [**histia**], *an invention as yet unknown to the men of those times, so as to take advantage of a favourable wind and outsail the oared fleet of Minos. Daedalus himself was saved, but the ship of Icarus is said to have overturned, as he was a clumsy helmsman* [**kubernōnti amathesteron**].[85]

According to this account, Daedalus invented sails, and Icarus died because he was a bad navigator.

Françoise Frontisi-Ducroux, in her discussion of this part of the Daedalus story,[86] stresses the intimate connection between navigation and flight and notes that the making of wings and the building of boats have much in common, with the careful fitting together of parts and the shaping of gentle curves essential in both cases.

Navigation, like the flight of Daedalus and Icarus, was guided by positions of the heavenly bodies,[87] and moreover the Greeks understood the speeding of boats across the water in terms of flight, for Hesiod instructs the navigator to "stow away the wings [*ptera*] of the sea-going ship neatly" at the end of the season "when the Pleiades plunge into the misty sea."[88] These *ptera* might be the boat's sails, whose invention Pausanias credits Daedalus with, an equation which, as Sarah P. Morris points out, Hesiod makes explicit when he says that the Aeginetans "were the first to build ships, curved on both ends, and they first put up sails [*histia*], the wings [*ptera*] of a seagoing ship."[89] But a boat's *ptera* could just as easily be the "shapely oars [*euēre' eretma*]" that Homer, in the *Odyssey*, says are "as wings unto ships."[90]

Sails, at least when filled with wind, are certainly shaped like wings. But unlike wings, which are horizontal to a bird's body, sails project vertically from the body of the ship, and sails, moreover, do not move rhythmically as wings do. A single oar, on the other hand, or even a pair of oars bears little resemblance to birds' wings. But oars are, individually, shaped rather like feathers, and ancient Greek ships, at least the large, fast ones, were not propelled by a single pair of oars, any more than birds are by just two feathers. From the third millennium onward, the ships that plied the Mediterranean basin had *banks* of oars, projecting horizontally, like wings, from the body of the vessel, and consisting of anything from ten to thirty oars to a side. It is this assembly of oars that, like the feathers Daedalus collates with wax, together made an oared ship winged. When oarsmen plied their oars, the action, collectively, of their oars beating the water was virtually identical to that of bird wings beating the air in flight. Indeed, Daedalus advised his son to steer the middle course, because the lower regions of the air were believed to be thicker than the upper; more like water, in fact.[91]

The *ptera* of ships, whether sails or banks of oars, were what propelled them forward. Swift motion makes things winged, for the ships of the Phaeacians in the *Odyssey* are said to be "as swift as a wing [*pteron*] or as a thought [*noēma*]."[92] In Homer, spoken words, words that are addressed to someone, are winged words, *epea pteroenta*, a stock phrase that occurs repeatedly in the *Iliad*, the *Odyssey*, and the Homeric hymns. Spoken words are winged creatures that fly out across the barrier of the teeth (*herkos odontōn*). Arrows that "leap from the bow string"[93] are also *pteroenta*,[94] which has as much to do with the speed of their release from the tension between bent bow and taut string as with the fact that they are feathered. When Achilles tries on the armor made for him by Hephaestus to see if it fits, "his glorious limbs moved free, and it became like wings to him,"[95] a source of speed and strength.

Shipwrecked, or with wings dismembered by the heat of the sun, Icarus drowned because he was *kubernōnti amathesteron*—literally "more unlearned in steering," less skilled than his father, who had built both Labyrinth and *choros* and knew how to steer the middle course. So also did the wily Odysseus, who, like Daedalus, was possessed of *mētis*[96] (cleverness, skill), and was able, successfully, to steer his ship through the narrow strait between the man-devouring Scylla and the ship-swallowing whirlpool of Charybdis.[97]

The Western tradition has made the adolescent Icarus, with his defiance in daring to fly too high, the hero of the

Daedalus and Icarus, by Marie Briot.

story, to the point where the mature Daedalus who made the wings and used them skillfully has all but disappeared from our cultural memory. Themes involving grand gestures, pride and fall, **hybris** and its chastisement pervade Western literature. We are *made* to reach too high:

> Nature that fram'd us of four elements,
> Warring within our breasts for regiment,
> Doth teach us all to have aspiring minds.[98]

Or as Robert Browning would have it,

> Ah, but a man's reach should exceed his grasp
> Or what's a heaven for.[99]

It is the Ovidian[100] version of the story with its account of the fatal soar toward the sun that is at the root of Icarus' enduring prestige. The Icarus of the virtually forgotten navigation version, far from being a heroic symbol of doomed human aspiration, is an inept boy who cannot steer a boat properly. In the latter, probably more genuinely archaic variant of a legend that tells of a good navigator and a bad one, it is Daedalus who is the hero: Daedalus, whose credit is his skill in acknowledging danger and steering the middle course, not, like the Ovidian Icarus of tradition, rashly confronting danger head-on. It is revealing that the West has chosen to remember Ovid's Icarus, along with Ovid's chaos.

In the myth of Zas and Chthonie mentioned earlier, the world is made to appear through weaving, which, like flight, also has its counterpart in navigation. In the great contrapuntal theme of the *Odyssey*, Odysseus plies the seas to make a hitherto unknown world appear, while Penelope plies her loom in Ithaca.

Thanks to Lionel Casson's research on ancient boat building, it is possible to see how, when Odysseus builds his boat, the very technique he employs is a reflection of Penelope's as well. When properly understood, the way ancient shipwrights assembled their craft is clearly analogous to the technique of weaving. To edge-join planks with mortise-and-tenon joints is, essentially, to interlace pieces of wood. In the shipyard, planks laid in one direction were fastened to other planks by tenons that penetrated, or interlaced, the planks at right angles in order to bind them together. Similarly, on a loom, the warp threads (analogous to planks) extended in one direction are bound together by weft threads (analogous to tenons and pegs) traveling orthogonally, which interpenetrate the warp threads at right angles to make the cloth.

Histos, generically anything set upright,[101] is at once the mast of a ship and a Greek loom, which, like the mast, and unlike modern looms, was vertical rather than horizontal. *Histos* or *histion* is the web woven on the loom, and *histia* also are sails.

Furthermore, to build an ancient Greek boat or weave an ancient Greek textile was to create something that was essentially skin; something that, like the Homeric body (*chrōs*), was an *epiphaneia*: a surface and an appearing. "Textile" derives from the Latin *texere*, to weave, which in turn has its roots in all the Greek *tek-* words mentioned earlier: words that have to do not only with giving birth (*tiktein*) and skilled making of all kinds, but also, specifically, with the craft of the *tecton*, the carpenter or boat builder.

*Sing clear-voiced Muse, of Hephaestus famed for skill [**klutomētis**].
With bright-eyed Athene he taught men glorious crafts [**erga**] throughout the world—men who before used to dwell in caves in the mountains
like wild beasts. But now that they have learned crafts through Hephaestus famous for his art [**klutotechnēs**], easily they live a peaceful
life in their own houses the whole year round.*[102]

In the early Greek view, it was knowledge of crafts (**erga**) that
had brought humankind out of the bestial, into the civilized
state, for a craftsman was a **dēmioergos**. The word is a compound deriving from **dēmios**, public, belonging to the **dēmos**
(people and/or land, territory), and **ergon**, task, work, deed.
The essence of an **ergon**, work, is that it be productive. Like
the English word "work," **ergon** is both the process and the
product. Like the **kosmon** (arrang*ing*, arrange*ment*) discussed
earlier, **ergon** is both a gerund (work, as in work*ing*, what one
does) and a noun (a work, the result of what one does). When
Hephaestus, famed for his **mētis** and his **technē**, taught men
erga, he taught them not toilsome labor, which is process only,
but how to make things.[103]

As the hymn intimates, the result, globally, of **erga** is
civilization, community, the city. Thus, **dēmioergoi**, or **dēmiourgoi**, to adopt the more familiar, contracted, Attic spelling of
the word, are those whose work (thing made) is what is public,
what belongs to the people/land. They are those whose work
(productive work*ing*) lets the public realm appear.

Dēmiourgoi included not only craftsmen in the conven-
tional, modern sense whereby Daedalus is understood as a
craftsman. **Dēmiourgoi** were a whole class of people that in-

cluded heralds, prophets, doctors, bards, lawgivers, and magistrates, as well as builders. They formed, in the Homeric city, a kind of middle class, below the land-owning nobles and above the landless and tradeless *thetes*.[104] Like Daedalus and like Odysseus, they traveled, for as Homer says,

*Who, pray, of himself ever seeks out and bids a stranger from abroad, unless it be one of those that are **dēmioergoi**: a prophet [**mantis**], a healer of ills [**iētēra kakōn**], a builder [**tecton dourōn**], or a divine minstrel [**thespis aoidos**] who gives delight with his song? For these men are bidden all over the boundless earth [**apeiros gaia**].*[105]

The only strangers who were welcome in the ancient city were the itinerant *dēmiourgoi*, themselves not citizens, since craftsmen then, as now, could not actually share the identity of what they made. Rather, they were those through whose *erga* citizenship was made possible.

The cave-dwelling Cyclopes in the *Odyssey* are uncivilized because they have no assemblies (*agorai*) or laws, because they do not till the soil or raise flocks, and because they

have at hand no ships with vermilion cheeks [i.e., red-painted bows], nor are there shipwrights in their land who might build them well-benched[106] *ships, which should perform all their wants, passing to the cities of other folk, as men often cross the sea in ships to visit one another—craftsmen who would have made of this isle also a fair settlement.*[107]

The craftsman lets *kosmos* appear through the artifact. If we understand the craftsman as a *dēmiourgos* in the wider Greek sense of the term, yet retain the primordiality of the notion of craft in its more limited, physical sense, as the early Greeks did when they claimed that there was no community, no civilization, without such craft, then it becomes quite clear that the emergence of Greek politics—indeed of Western politics—hinged upon the craft tradition,[108] and upon how craft was understood. The *polis*, as we shall see, was understood and made as an artifact. Significantly enough, in Sparta the *agora* was called the *choros*, because, as Pausanias reports, it was the place where, at the *gymnopaidiai* (festival of naked boys), "which the Lacedamonians take more seriously than any other, the lads perform dances in honour of Apollo."[109] It would appear that, for the Spartans at least, the fact that their *agora* was a dancing place took precedence over other considerations.

Choros, moreover, is not only dance and dancing place. *Choros*, in what is perhaps its most familiar application, is also the *group* that dances, as in the chorus of a Greek tragedy. But *choros* can be, simply, any group, as for example when Herodotus speaks of the "band of a hundred youths" (*choron neēniōn hekaton*) sent by the Chians to Delphi.[110] *Choros*, in this generic sense, is people doing something together, a group with a shared purpose. People, one might say, who are in the same boat.

It is worth recalling the *choros* passage from the *Odyssey* cited earlier.

*Then stood up the masters of the lists [**aisymnētai**], nine in all, men chosen from among the people [**dēmioi**], who in their gatherings were wont to order all things aright. They levelled a dancing-place [**choros**] and marked out a fair wide ring . . .*[111]

The *aisymnētai* who in Homer organize dances and games in festivals were, in Asia Minor, a political body who were not actually council members but who, as the masters of convention, or guardians of propriety, eventually became the supreme magistrature (*archē*) in many Ionian towns.[112]

The political status of the *dēmiourgoi* declined in the classical era, and with it the whole notion of allowing *kosmos* to emerge through making. In the mid-fifth century B.C., Hippodamus of Miletus,[113] the alleged inventor of orthogonal planning, who "cut up [*katetemen*]"[114] the Piraeus during the Periclean period, and the "first man not engaged in politics who attempted to speak on the subject of the best form of constitution,"[115] advocated a population divided into three classes, one of artisans, one of farmers, and one of the military. But the word used for artisan, at least in Aristotle's account, is *technitēs* (artificer or skilled workman), not *dēmiourgos*. Although given by Hippodamus a place in the political order, the craftsman was no longer seen to make it. And for all that Plato's cosmos is made by a *dēmiourgos* in the *Timaeus*, Plato systematically downgrades the craftsman in his work.

Even so, it was under Pericles that the temple dedicated to Hephaestus was built on the western edge of the Athenian *agora*, on a site previously occupied by potters and bronzesmiths.[116] And it was on the edges of this same *agora* that Athenian artisans of the classical period continued to maintain their workshops. This was not simply a question of convenient access to the marketplace where artisans sold their wares. Like the *agora* itself, the workshops, recognized meeting places for discussion, were an important part of the public realm. Socrates himself is supposed to have had certain conversations in one or another of them.[117] Although the artisans themselves may, by the classical period, have ceased to be **dēmiourgoi** in the sense discussed, the location of their workshops and the role these played were, like the location of the temple of their patron Hephaestus, a testimony to a remembered interdependence of craft and community, of **erga** and the city.

The political dimension of craft is made explicit in the Daedalus legend, for when Daedalus reached Sicily after his escape from Crete "he built a city [**polin kateskeuase**] which lay upon a rock and was the strongest of any in Sicily, and altogether impregnable to any attack by force."[118] If the story is read historically—and this is entirely possible—it can be seen as a kind of epitome of the development of early Greek culture. In Athens, at the beginning of his career, Daedalus made statues, in Crete he built the Labyrinth and **choros**, and in Sicily, where the Greeks founded many colonial cities in the eighth and seventh centuries, Daedalus built a city.

In what, as Sarah P. Morris points out, is an extension of Daedalus' adventures in Sicily, Diodorus Siculus tells of a visit to neighboring Sardinia where its ruler, Iolaus, has sent for him:

And having sent for Daedalus from Sicily, he built many great works which have survived until now and are called "Daidaleia" from his construction of them. He built not only gymnasia, large and elegant, but also established law courts and other things promoting well-being [**eudaimoniē**, *literally "good divine power"*].[119]

IV
Between Movement
and Fixity:
The Place for Order

It has so far been my argument that the theoretical event, so called, of sixth-century Greece hinged upon an emergent awareness of order whose **genesis**, whose coming-to-be, was rooted in the early Greek perception of craft as the revelation of **kosmos**. The work of the carpenter revealed it through cutting and assembly, the textile embodied it through the rhythms of a shuttle moving over a loom, the dancing floor was its appearing in the dance, and the boat, which sped through the waves like a bird through the air, made it manifest through both its building and its navigation. The first articulation of this order was Anaximander's, but its discovery was that of Daedalus, and if Daedalus was the mythical first architect, it is through the Daedalus legend that the architectural beginnings of Western thinking are to be understood.

 The **Polis**

In his book *La naissance de la cité grecque: cultes, espace et société VIII–VII siècles avant J.-C.*, a work based on recent archaeological research, François de Polignac presents evidence for the formative role of what he calls *la cité cultuelle*, or ritual city, in the emergence of the Greek **polis**. Athens, he stresses, was not, as is usually assumed, the paradigm but rather the exception, being, with its centralized structure focused on the Acropolis, something of a unique survivor from the Mycenaean period and its palace cultures. The typical cases were the other Greek cities—among them the cities of Asia Minor, and also, especially, the colonial cities of Sicily, Magna Graecia, and the Black Sea area—which only emerged in the eighth and seventh centuries, after the so-called "dark age" (twelfth to ninth centuries) that followed the Dorian invasion and the subsequent collapse of Mycenaean civilization.

Irad Malkin, in his study of religion and Greek colonization, is vociferous in the defense of the rationally or functionally planned, as opposed to the emergent, or what I would call "made," city, citing the case of Greek colonial foundations as evidence.[1] He also suggests that "colonialization contributed just as much towards the rise of the *polis* as it was dependent on this rise for its own existence."[2] I cannot agree that the colonial founders were urban planners, as Malkin's argument suggests. The regularity of street layouts Malkin brings to bear as evidence seems to me to have much more to do with the notion of allowing *kosmos* to appear through their rhythm than with planning in the modern sense of the word. However, his argument for a reciprocal relationship between the development of *polis* and colonial city is convincing. Furthermore such reciprocity has important implications with respect to the role navigation and ships played in the making and thinking of the new *poleis*. If the colonial foundations influenced the emergent *poleis* as much as vice versa, the fact that Greek colonists were all, necessarily, sailors before they became settlers becomes very significant. Between the *metropolis*, or mother city, and the new foundation, the city existed as a ship.

Weaving the City

What is noteworthy about the new *poleis*, in contrast to the old Mycenaean cities, is the presence of sanctuaries, which had never existed in the Mycenaean civilization, apart from the hearth of the quasi-divine king-father within the Mycenaean palaces themselves. There are tombs at Mycenae and Knossos, but no temples. François de Polignac carefully maps the archaeological traces of the eighth- and seventh-century sanctuaries and shows how they fall into three categories:[3] urban sanctuaries, within the inhabited urban area itself; suburban sanctuaries, placed at the limit of, or at a short distance from, the habitat; and extraurban sanctuaries, which were not part of daily ritual, since they were located some six to twelve kilometers from the town at the very limit of the city's territory (*chōra*). Many of the most celebrated sanctuaries of the Greek world are indeed located on nonurban sites, and in view of this, it is impossible to maintain that the city grew up around the temple, which is the conclusion drawn if Athens, mistakenly, is taken as paradigmatic.

Rather, it would appear to be possible to extrapolate from de Polignac's argument the notion of a *polis* allowed to appear as a surface woven by the activity of its inhabitants: the sequential building of sanctuaries over a period of time, which at times stretched over decades, and the subsequent ritual processions from center to urban limit to territorial limit and back again, in what can be seen as a kind of Ariadne's dance, magnified to cover a territory that was not called *choros* but *chōra*.[4]

In the *Iliad* *chōrē*, which is the Ionic form of *chōra*, is a scant space (*oligē chōrē*) between, such as that between a horse and a chariot,[5] or the one in which the corpse of Patroclus is dragged to and fro[6] after Hector has slain him, or the narrow rim of shoreline left for the Achaeans to fight in.[7] The verb *chōreō* is used in the military sense of giving ground before the enemy.[8]

Chōros,[9] the masculine form of *chōra* or *chōrē*, in general denotes a space that is somewhat more defined than the feminine *chōra*. In one notable passage Hector and Odysseus "measured out a [masculine] space [*chōron diemetreon*]"[10] for the single combat between Paris and Menelaus, who then "took their stand near together in the measured space [*diametrētōi eni chōrōi*]."[11] Relevant in this context is the so-called Pyrrhic dance that was part of every Spartan soldier's military training.

In the *Odyssey*, where the word, more often than not, appears in its masculine, *chōros*, form, the tendency is for it to mean place as location,[12] but also land, country, or territory. According to the Aristotelian definition, *chōra*, translated by Loeb as "room," is similar to place (*topos*), which Aristotle says is a "surface-continent [*epipedon periechon*] that encompasses its content in the manner of a vessel."[13] *Chōra* is different from void (*kenon* or *chaos*, which Aristotle equates and says do not exist).

Now it is, of course, very dangerous to read backward from Aristotle into the archaic period.[14] However, Aristotle's discussion of *topos* and *chōra* does suggest a possible guess as to how the *chōra* of the *polis* may have been understood in earlier times as a territory made to appear through a continual remaking, or reweaving of its encompassing surface, just as the world itself was made to appear when the colonists' ships plied the seas.

In the same chapter of his *Physics*, Aristotle notes[15] that Plato too identified *topos* and *chōra* in the *Timaeus*. Plato says that after the "first kind," which is "self-identical form [*eidos*], ungenerated and indestructible," and the "second kind," the object perceptible by sense "becoming in a place [*topōi*] and out of it again perishing,"[16] is a "third kind":

*. . . ever-existing place [**chōra**] which admits not of destruction and provides room for all things that have birth, itself being apprehensible by a kind of bastard reasoning by the aid of non-sensation, barely an object of belief; for . . . it is somehow necesssary that all that exists should exist in some spot [**en tini topōi**] and occupying some place [**ketachon chōron tina**] and that that which is neither on earth nor anywhere in the heaven is nothing.*[17]

Plato's **chōra**, the receptacle of Becoming, is eternal and indestructible, but the **chōra** of the nascent, archaic **polis** was not. The archaic **polis** was an uncertain place that needed to be anchored at the strategic points of center, middle ground, and outer limit by the new sanctuaries. It was not a vessel with a fixed form, but, like the appearing surface of a woven cloth—of all the traces of material culture one of the most perishable—had continually to be mended or made to reappear.

And why, to return to the question that has long vexed historians of urban form, were the streets of colonial foundations regularly spaced? Why did they intersect at right angles? I suggested earlier, a little vaguely, that their regularity had to do with **kosmos**, but if we think of the city in terms of weaving, as I believe the early Greeks did, the intention made manifest in orthogonal street layouts becomes quite precise. Weaving, says H. Ling Roth,[18] "consists of the interlacing *at right angles* [my italics] by one series of filaments or threads, known as the weft . . . of another series, known as the warp, both being in the same plane." **Harmonia**, close fitting, can be a feature of the tightly woven cloth only: a textile with a loose weave is not, so to speak, "harmonious." It does not, properly speaking, appear at all. And one cannot produce a "harmonious," tightly woven fabric if warp and weft threads are not regularly spaced and are not at right angles to one another, perfectly orthogonal. Nor, for that matter, could an ancient Greek shipwright build a watertight boat if the tenons were not at right angles to the planks. In a textile, skewed or unequally distributed threads produce a loosely woven fabric full of holes, just as in a boat skewed tenons make for a leaky vessel. This was the last thing the people who founded new Greek cities in strange, often hostile lands would have wanted.

In the mid-fifth century, the Piraeus was given an orthogonal "plan" whose traces today have all but disappeared. One supposes, however, that the configuration of this plan must have been at least generically similar to the plan of Selinous, the seventh-century colonial foundation in Sicily whose plan is illustrated here, even though Hippodamian planning is usually considered to be based on a square grid.

Now the Piraeus was, as it still remains, the port of Athens, and ports, generally speaking, are populated by shifty characters of every description. Being places where people continually come and go, they are not known for having a "harmonious" or coherent urban fabric. The habitués of ports do not form closely knit communities. The Piraeus of the mid-fifth century was no exception. Practically waterless, with steep, barren hills, it also had an unhealthy climate due to its proximity to the Halipedon Marsh.[19] By the Periclean period it was full of foreigners, who practiced strange, extravagant Great Mother cults.[20] As the largest and most populous deme of Athens, it had also become a hotbed of radical democracy. Everything about the Piraeus lacked *harmonia*: its climate, its topography, its population. Thus when, at Pericles' request, Hippodamus of Miletus "cut up" the Piraeus and imposed an

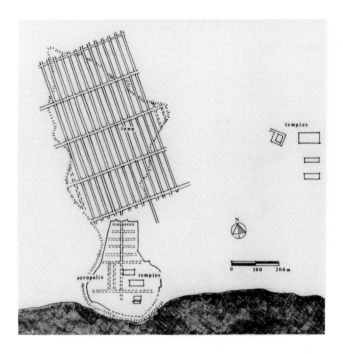

*Plan of Selinous, a Greek colony in Sicily
founded in 627 B.C.*

orthogonal grid of streets on its very difficult existing terrain, the intention would have been to make the Piraeus "harmonious," the way a well-built boat or a tightly woven cloth was understood by the early Greeks to be "harmonious"—even as in earlier centuries the founders of colonial cities had sought to ensure the *harmonia* of their new foundations by laying out regularly spaced streets that intersected at right angles.

The Piraeus was something like a colonial foundation in more ways than just this one. Hippodamus' "cutting up" took place a generation after Themistocles had had, as Thucydides puts it, "the audacity to suggest that the Athenians should attach themselves to the sea [*tēs thalassēs anthektea*]."[21] Themistocles, by building the Piraeus as the Athenian port and laying the foundations of Athens' sea power, made Athens a *metropolis*, a mother city. Graphically umbilical long walls, also built at this time, linked the "child" to its mother and underscored the maternal connection.[22] And just as the parental relation between mother cities and their colonial foundations became reciprocal to become manifest in the rise of the *polis*, so did the roles of Athens and the Piraeus become reversed, for by sustaining the city with imported goods the port became the nurturing mother of the city that had given it birth. As Plutarch, who calls Athens' sea empire the mother of democracy, says, "Themistocles did not, as Aristophanes the comic poet says, 'knead the Piraeus onto the city,' nay, he fastened the city to the Piraeus and the land to the sea."[23]

It has been argued, chiefly by Joseph Rykwert, that orthogonal street layouts had to do with orientation: with squaring the position of the citizen with the geometric configuration of the cosmos. This certainly seems to be so. But in early Greece, where craftsmen were known as *dēmiourgoi*, and before either the cosmos or city streets became geometrical, the experience of weavers had already led them to the discovery that the *kosmos* of a tightly woven cloth depended on equally spacing warp and weft threads and interlacing them at right angles to one another.

When Irad Malkin discusses the choosing of sites for the new sanctuaries in colonial cities, he refers, as evidence for the colonial founders' functional approach, to a certain passage

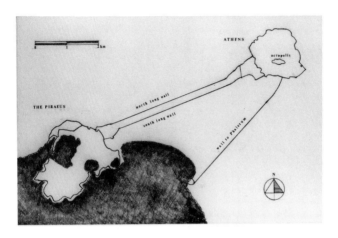

Athens, the Piraeus, and the long walls.

from Aristotle's *Politics*. The Barker translation of this passage reads as follows.

*This site [**topos**] should be on an eminence conspicuous [**epiphaneia**] enough for men to look up and see goodness [**aretē**] enthroned [**ikanōs**] and strong enough [**erymnoterōs**] to command [**geitniōnta**] the ad-jacent quarters [**merē**] of the city.*[24]

"This conspicuousness," says Malkin, "seems straightforward and signifies prominence and impressiveness . . . as a criterion for choosing the site of a sacred area." A close look at the original Greek[25] reveals nothing so straightforward. First of all, in the Greek there is not one word about looking up, or about the *topos* being "on an eminence": these are the translator's interpolations. Secondly, *epiphaneia*, a word already discussed at some length, has only a secondary relationship to conspicuousness. **Epiphaneia** has to do with appearing, visibility being the evidence for existence: *epiphaneia* is visible surface, and testifies to coming-to-light. That *epiphaneia* should be read as "prominence and impressiveness" is also an interpolation. Thirdly, **aretē**, goodness, is **ikanōs**, which is not to say "enthroned" but reached, fulfilled, or attained in a becoming or appropriate way. And, finally, **geitniōnta** is a participle of the verb **geinomai**: to be born.

Thus, a legitimate alternative reading of the passage might be: "The place should be such as to have **epiphaneia** so as to see goodness fulfilled and strengthened, so that the regions of the city might come to be." If a city is to be woven, **hyphainein** (brought to light), so that it may appear (have **epiphaneia**), the sites for the temples whose building is integral to that city's appearing must also, themselves, have **epiphaneia**. And if Aristotle's view on the choosing of temple locations can be taken to bear traces of how these sites were in fact chosen in the early colonial cities, it is a view which, when read with an effort to think Greek rather than functional modern, entirely sustains what I have been attempting to articulate about the weaving of the city.

The colonial founder's authority came from the Delphic oracle, which is to say from the god Phoebus Apollo, "and Phoebus it is that men follow when they measure [**diemetrē-santo**] cities; for Phoebus evermore delights in the founding of cities, and Phoebus himself weaves [**hyphainei**] their foundations."[26] Hephaestus, as the hymn cited earlier suggests, taught men **erga**, the crafts that made possible the existence of human communities. The hymn also mentions Athena: "With bright-eyed [**glaukōpis**][27] Athena he taught men glorious crafts." The craft specific to Hephaestus, god of the forge, was metalworking. The craft specific to Athena, goddess of the city, was weaving. Athena, patroness of all cities, but chiefly of course of Athens, taught people how to weave. If it was Apollo who masterminded colonial expeditions and wove the foundations of cities, it was Athena, bright-eyed patroness, also, of weavers, who taught people how to make these cities visible.

The **Peplos** of Athena

Athens, it has been noted, was the exception among Greek city-states because, as a centralized survivor from the Mycenaean period, it had not emerged through the building of extraurban sanctuaries by immigrant populations[28] as the other Greek cities had. The Athenians, Pericles stresses in the funeral oration, were autochthonous: ". . . this land [*chōra*] of ours in which the same people have never ceased to dwell in an unbroken line of successive generations . . ."[29] Or as Herodotus has the Athenian envoys to Syracuse say, the Athenians "can show of all the longest lineage, and . . . alone among the Greeks have never changed their dwelling."[30]

When Pericles' predecessor, Themistocles, had "the audacity to suggest that the Athenians should attach themselves to the sea . . . in so doing [he] lay the basis for their empire [*archē*]."[31] With this attachment to the sea, accomplished by the building of the long walls that connected Athens to its port, Athens became a sea power and the receptacle for the wealth of Hellas, which included not only grain and gold but people, both craftsmen, who formed the core of the resident alien population of metics, and thinkers from Ionia, by then overrun by the Persians.

*The folded **peplos** of Athena,*
Parthenon east frieze, mid-fifth century B.C.

It was only then, in the classical period, that, according to François de Polignac, the Athenians began to develop their nonurban sanctuaries.[32] Athens, initially, had not been woven, the way the new city-states were. The Mycenaean city was a preexisting dancing place (*choros*), or fixed receptacle (*chōra*) for the fifth-century Athenian *polis* made to appear through a dance that had been discovered elsewhere.[33]

The memory of this dance was preserved in the festival of Athena, in the yearly Lesser (*mikra*) Panathenaea and the Great (*megala*) Panathenaea that took place every four years. Scholars disagree as to which were yearly and which only four-yearly events in the unfolding of the ritual, but the general outline of the festival, as it took place in classical times, is as follows.

Nine months before the feast, on the festival of Chalkeia, which was the feast of Hephaestus, the patron of craftsmen, two of the four *arrephoroi*, priestesses of Athena, initiated the weaving (*hyphainein*) of a new *peplos*, or robe, to clothe the ancient wooden statue (*archaion agalma*) of the goddess, whose name, Athena, Karl Kerényi has suggested, may be linked to certain very old words for different kinds of receptacles.[34] The draperies of this primitive, olive wood image were not carved, as they were on the colossal gold and ivory Athena of the Periclean period made by Phidias, nor were any of the other items of her apparel. These included a crown (*stephanē*), a neck band (*ochthoibos*), five necklaces, a golden aegis, and a golden gorgoneion (head of Medusa, possibly attached to the aegis). In her hand she held a golden libation bowl (*phialē*). Somewhere in the ensemble there figured a golden owl.[35] Pausanias, whose description of Phidias' celebrated statue is detailed but expresses no particular reverence,[36] says nothing about the appearance of the more ancient statue, except to note with awe "the most holy thing [*hagiōstaton*] . . . is the image of Athena which is on what is now called the Acropolis but in early days [was called] the *polis*. A legend concerning it says that it fell from heaven."[37]

The Panathenaea usually lasted for four days and began on the final days of the lunar cycle, continuing through the moon's disappearance and culminating at the appearance of the new moon,[38] with the famous Panathenaean procession immortalized in the frieze that surrounded the *naos* of the Parthenon. The procession (*pompē*) began at sunrise with the participation of the entire Athenian populace. It set out from the Cerameicus, the deme of Athens adjoining the Dipylon Gate, proceeded to Eleusis, and then returned to the Acropolis.[39]

The new *peplos* was spread like a sail above a car either constructed like a boat or one that was indeed a boat, which must have been mounted on wheels. Pausanias mentions a Panathenaic ship that was noted for its speed.[40] The ancient wooden image of Athena Polias, by classical times located in the Erectheion, was clothed in her new robe, and there followed the sacrifice of cattle and the sharing of the flesh of the victims among the people, with further celebrations that included dancing and other contests.

The meaning of all this, in the light of everything discussed so far, is transparent: the nine months' gestation of the new *peplos* which was a woven surface-appearing, an *epiphaneia*; the festival whose culmination coincided with the epiphany of the new moon ("much *kosmos* arises from her shining light");[41] the *peplos* that, before it clothed the statue, was the sail of a swift ship in the *pompē* in which the Athenian people remade the city by weaving their way from the Cerameicus, known for the manufacture of pottery vessels, to Eleusis and back to the Acropolis; the reappearance or rebirth, through her being clothed, of bright-eyed (*glaukōpis*) Athena, who is accompanied by her owl (*glaux*), a bird known for its ability to see in the dark; and, of course, the dances—the *kyklikoi choroi*—and the sacrificial meal that together reaffirmed community.

The *peplos* was the central feature of the feast, as the position of the relief illustrating the presentation to Athena of her new robe stresses: it is located directly above the entrance to the temple where it appears as the focus of the entire Parthenon frieze.

In the *Iliad*, Hecuba offers to the Athena of the Trojan citadel a new *peplos*, among the *peploi* in her treasure chest, "the one that was fairest in its weaving [*poikilmasin*] and amplest, and shone like a star."[42] With her offering, Hecuba begs the goddess to save Troy. "'Take pity on Troy and the Trojans' wives and their little children.' So spoke she praying, but Pallas Athene denied her prayer."[43] Athena was not swayed by Hecuba's gift of the *peplos*, the city ceased its appearing, and Troy was destroyed.

Ships and City

"Well-walled Troy," "great city of Priam," was denied Athena's favor, and Troy perished. The Achaeans, however, were granted her support. It is clear that the fleet of Achaean ships beached at the mouth of the Meander during the ten-year siege of Troy was thought of as a city, for in Book VII of the *Iliad* the Achaeans

Warship: sealstone intaglio, ca. 500 B.C.
The "bossed" shields of the hoplites on deck might be noted.

built a wall and a lofty rampart, a defence for their ships and for themselves. And therein they made gates close-fastening, that through them might be a way for the driving of chariots . . . and the gods . . . marvelled at the great work of the bronze-coated Achaeans.[44]

Among the Achaeans, Athena had two special favorites. One of them was Achilles, whose dragging of Hector's naked corpse by the heels around the walls of Troy signaled the city's ultimate destruction. The other was Odysseus of the many wiles, boat builder and expert navigator.

The transcription of the *Odyssey* dates from a period of colonization that saw, and influenced, the rise of the **polis**; a period when colonists, all, were sailors first. Thus, the account of Odysseus' long sea voyage in the second Homeric epic can be read poetically as the weaving of another city,[45] a **polis**, which, like the open city of the Phaeacians, "famed for their ships,"[46] where all is harmonious, all *eu kata kosmon*, is entirely different in nature from that of the monolithic, impregnable Trojan citadel.

For the new city-states François de Polignac describes, the cities that emerged in the eighth and seventh centuries, were, ultimately, the cities of Achaean navigators: both the cities of Greek Asia Minor and the colonies these cities in turn founded throughout the Mediterranean basin and around the Black Sea.

Theseus, who, according to legend, united the scattered Attic communities and, as the mythical founder of the Athenian **polis**, transformed Athens from a Mycenaean citadel into a city-state, was also a sailor. As a youth he sailed to Crete, where he slew the Minotaur and found his way out of the Labyrinth. A long sea voyage brought him back to Athens, and there, according to Plutarch, his ship was preserved as a sacred relic.

The ship wherein Theseus and the youth of Athens returned had thirty oars, and was preserved by the Athenians down even to the time of Demetrius Phalereus,[47] for they took away the old planks as they decayed, putting in new and stronger timber in their place, in so much that the ship became a standing example among the philosophers, for the logical question of things that grow; one side holding that the ship remained the same, and the other contending that it was not the same.[48]

It is perhaps this very ship to which Plato refers at the opening of the *Phaedo*.[49] As Plato tells it, it was the yearly sacred voyage of Theseus' alleged ship to Delos and back, during which time "the city must be pure and no one may be publicly executed," that caused the lengthy delay between Socrates' trial and execution.

It was Theseus too who, according to Thucydides, Pausanias, and Plutarch, instituted the Panathenaea, although other authorities date its inception, historically, to the sixth century or even later.[50] As we saw, in the early fifth century Athens attached herself to the sea. Only after this did Theseus, before then a minor hero in Attic legend, begin to figure largely in the Athenian self-consciousness. It was not until the fifth century, after Cimon "found" the bones of Theseus on the island of Skiros and brought them to Athens to be buried in the agora,[51] that the cult of Theseus became a state cult.[52]

A ship, even in current English usage, is a vessel (container, receptacle), and Homeric ships, which according to Lionel Casson had no decks, are almost invariably referred to as "hollow." Moreover, we continue to speak of the "ship of state," and as Alberti was to note in the fifteenth century, "The ancients . . . compared the city to a ship on the high seas constantly exposed to accidents and danger, through the negligence of its citizens and the envy of its neighbors."[53] The emblem of Paris, where nature, with the help of the city's builders, has conspired to make its Île de la Cité boat-shaped, is a ship.

At one important point in its history Athens literally became a fleet of ships. When Themistocles evacuated Athens in 481 B.C. in the face of the Persian threat, the entire city put out to sea, taking with it its **archaion agalma** of Athena Polias. And when, according to Plutarch, a certain person said to Themistocles "that a man without a city had no business to advise men who still had cities of their own" Themistocles answered,

It is true thou wretch, that we have left behind us our houses and our city walls, not deeming it meet for the sake of such lifeless things to be in subjection; but we still have a city, the greatest in Hellas, our two hundred triremes. [54]

The Athenian attachment to the sea did not sit well with Socrates, who, as we saw, objected to things that move around. In the *Gorgias*, he links the political decline of Athens directly to its emergence as a sea power:

You praise the men who feasted the citizens and satisfied their desires, and people say that they have made the city great not seeing that the swollen and ulcerated condition of the State is to be attributed to these elder statesmen, [55] *for they have filled the city full of harbours and docks and walls* [56] *and revenues and all that, and have left no room for justice and temperance.* [57]

According to Plutarch, it was in the last years of the fifth century, during the oligarchy of the Thirty, that the tyrants (whom Socrates, to his subsequent discredit, never opposed)[58] turned the speaker's platform of the Pnyx around so that it faced the land rather than the sea. The gesture was at once antidemocratic and antimaritime since, as Plutarch tells it, it was Themistocles' development of the Piraeus that had

*increased the privileges of the common people [**ton dēmon**] as against the nobles [**tōn aristōn**], and filled them with boldness since the controlling power came now into the hands of skippers and boatswains and pilots. Therefore it was, too, that the bema in Pnyx, which had stood so as to look off toward the sea, was afterwards turned by the thirty tyrants so as to look inland, because they thought that maritime empire was the mother of democracy [**dēmocratia**].* [59]

It would, of course, be simpleminded to read Plato's *Republic* or his *Laws* as blueprints for an ideal political order, but the notion is undeniably implicit in the very existence of such writings that political order could be *thought* without being *made*. Boats have no place in the **polis** of Plato's *Laws*, which is to be located eighty stades away from the sea, a distance that, as Robert Garland has pointed out, is exactly twice the distance of Athens from the Piraeus.[60]

Plato continues to see dancing as primordial, however, for without a "perception of the various kinds of order and disorder in movement, which we term rhythm [**rhythmos**] and harmony," there is no understanding of community or political order. "The uneducated man," says Plato, "is without choir-training [**achoreutos**], and the educated man fully choir-trained [**kekchoreukota**],"[61] and since choir training embraces both dancing and song, "the well-educated man must be able both to sing and dance well."[62]

In classical Athens, the memory of emerging order was reenacted in the Panathenaea, and preserved in the dance. Although it was a living memory, rich with shared meaning, the age of discovery was over.

 The Peripteral Temple

The emergence of the Greek **polis** in the eighth and seventh centuries as what François de Polignac has called a *cité cultuelle* was indissociable from the building of sanctuaries, and the salient, central feature of these sanctuaries was usually, although not always, the temple. At first a freestanding **megaron**,[63] it very soon afterward became the prototypical "Greek" temple, with its **naos**, the dwelling place of the cult statue, surrounded by a peristyle of evenly spaced columns. When, in the eighth and seventh centuries, the Greek temple became peripteral, it acquired **ptera**, wings.[64]

The Heraion at Samos

The temple of Hera at Samos, located, by de Polignac's classification, at the limit of the territory of the **polis**, was among the first temples to become winged.[65] The earliest structure, built in the late ninth or early eighth century, was the first **hecatompedon**, or one-hundred-foot-long temple, with mud brick walls, whose pitched roof, spanning a width of twenty feet, was supported by an axial row of interior pillars. It was not long after this, toward the middle of the eighth century, that the columns, wooden ones resting on circular stone bases, came outside: seventeen on each of the long sides, seven across the front, and six at the back, with the roof extended to cover them.

Various formal or functional reasons have been proposed for the setting of this momentous precedent. According to J. N. Coldstream, the peristyle was a "lavish and spectacular method of protecting the mud-brick walls against the elements."[66] In a similar vein, Jeffrey Hurwit claims that "the colonnade was meant above all to impress," adding however (not unwisely, but with no further elaboration) that the temple so enlarged gave "physical expression and focus to belief, purpose and community."[67] J. J. Coulton says,

The portico does not appear to have any structural value, and with a depth of only 1.30 m. it could not provide much useful shelter for visiting pilgrims; nor could it have had much religious significance to

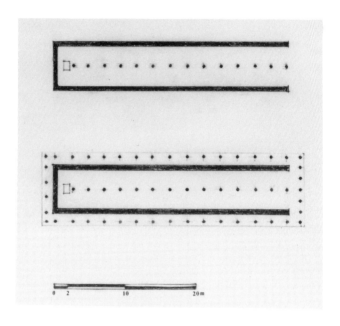

*Plans of the two phases of the first temple of Hera at Samos,
eighth century B.C.*

*any eighth-century Greek. Perhaps it was inspired by the frequent
mention of porticoes in epic descriptions of palaces.*[68]

Vincent Scully says that the peristyle was intended "to articulate, penetrate, and extend the exterior envelope of the building so that it should become a true mid-space element, at once
bounded and boundless . . . setting up with its columns . . . a
regular standard of measure whereby distant horizons could be
grasped."[69] These comments are fundamentally convincing, and
are reflected, to a certain extent, by some of the concerns

Between Movement and Fixity

expressed in this essay. But in the last analysis I do not think the early Greeks were capable of thinking in such abstract, formal terms.

The Heraion at Samos was the home of the cult image of Hera, a *xoanon* that was kept chained up in order to reveal the fearful dynamism of its divine life. The first mud brick Heraion, with its interior hearth place, was a house writ large, and it is in the nature of houses with their hearths to be fixed, to be anchored to the soil.

Hestia, the hearth,[70] is a feminine noun linked to the verb *histēmi*, I set up, a link that is further stressed by the Ionian spelling of *hestia* as *histia*. But *histia* (neuter plural) are also sails, as noted earlier. Also linked to the verb *histēmi*, and as essential to the constitution of every Greek household as its hearth, was the loom. A Greek loom was not horizontal but set upright, and was called a *histon*. So was the mast of a ship.

Everything in the Hellas of those early centuries was on the move; not only in the divine world of gods and deathless *physis*, but also in the human world (at the time, not yet wholly separate from the divine), with the new cities and their emerging political order, and the swift ships that set out on colonizing expeditions, carrying in their hollow hulls the hearth fires of mother cities to far-flung destinations all over the known world.[71]

And so, in the very image of the *polis* as it was being newly made, and of whose making it was such an essential feature, the shrine (*naos*) of the goddess became a ship (*naus*)[72] with "well-fitted oars [*euēre' eretma*] that are as wings unto ships."[73] The cult statue was tied down because it was, essentially, mobile. The temple was given mobility because it had been, essentially, fixed.

It is worth recalling, in this context, that Icarus, whether shipwrecked or unwinged, was in all the accounts drowned near Samos. Among the craftsmen for which that island was justly famous in archaic times[74] is Theodorus of Samos, who, with his father Rhoikos, built the mid-sixth-century temple of Hera at Samos mentioned by Vitruvius.[75] Theodorus was also, with Chersiphron and Metagenes, architect of the temple of Artemis at Ephesus, on the Ionian mainland not far from Samos. These two shrines, built on a scale rarely surpassed since, were the first dipteral temples.

Why, in the sixth century, did Greek temples acquire *two* sets of wings? The earliest oared ships were long and narrow, with single banks of oars, just like the first peripteral Heraion. Sometime in the late eighth century, it was discovered that two banks of oars made for more compact, sturdier, and more seaworthy ships.[76] Furthermore, as Lionel Casson notes, "when in 704 B.C., the island of Samos decided to create a navy, it applied to Corinth and the latter sent it a topflight architect who superintended the construction of four vessels of the latest design, probably two-banked galleys."[77] If, when temples acquired wings, **naos** became **naus**, it would have been only natural for the shrine so outfitted to keep step with the evolution of its model.

Theodorus is also credited with the invention of the level and of the lathe, as well as with building a labyrinth at Lemnos. Indeed, even the dipteral Heraion, with its 104 columns, seems to have been understood as labyrinthine, for when Pliny the Elder speaks of Theodorus he calls him the builder of "the labyrinth at Samos."[78] Theodorus, moreover, is seen as something of a historical counterpart to the mythical Daedalus,[79] and Plato couples Theodorus not only with Daedalus but also

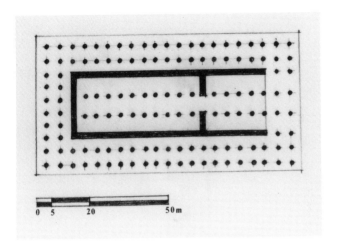

The third, dipteral temple of Hera at Samos,
by Rhoikos and Theodoros (570–540 B.C.).

with Epeius, builder of the Trojan horse.[80] Admittedly, Theodorus did not build the first winged temple at Samos: it
predated him by at least two hundred years. But the curious
correspondences between the mythical and historical figures
further suggest that the ***pteron*** of the peripteral temple had
much to do with an early understanding of architecture both
as embodied flight and as navigation.

Furthermore, this is how Pausanias describes the tradition concerning the origins of the temple of Apollo at Delphi:

*They say that the most ancient temple of Apollo was made of
laurel. . . . This temple must have had the form of a hut. The Delphians
say that the second temple was made by bees from bees-wax and
feathers, and that it was sent to the Hyperboreans by Apollo. Another*

story is current, that the temple was set up by a Delphian, whose name was Pteras, and so the temple received its name from the builder.[81]

The builder of the second, wax-and-feather temple at Delphi was Pteras, "winged man," and, as noted earlier, the assembly of feather-shaped oars in the banks of a galley is what made the boat winged. Françoise Frontisi-Ducroux, who invokes the foregoing passage from Pausanias, also mentions a mutilated passage in Pindar that might arguably be construed as describing this second temple as having been built by Daedalus.[82] It need hardly be added that, like almost all the great temples of the period, the sixth-century temple of Apollo at Delphi was peripteral.

The city became a ship, its **naos** a **naus**, with well-fitted oars like wings. Although not all temples had **ptera**, only temples had them. The temple, like a ship, had a prow, a front, a *fronton*, for as characteristic of the Greek temple as its **pteron** is its triangular gable end or pediment: in Greek, its **aetos**, its eagle,[83] so called, according to Galen, because of a gable's resemblance to outspread wings.[84] Unlike the ships of the Phoenicians, called **hippoi** because of their horse head prows, the prows of early Greek ships did not carry figureheads.[85] But in Hellenistic representations it is on the prows of boats that **nikai**, victories, alight, with wings outspread.[86]

Eurythmia

In Book I, Chapter 2 of *De Architectura*, Vitruvius discusses the things on which architecture depends.[87] The terms Vitruvius uses are mostly Greek. These are **taxis** (order), **diathesis** (ar-

Nike of Samothrace. After 306 B.C.

rangement), decor, distribution, "which in Greek is called *oe-conomia*," and *eurythmia*. *Eurythmia*, says Vitruvius,

> *implies a graceful semblance; the suitable display of details* [membra]
> *in their context. This is attained when the details of the work are of a*
> *height suitable to their breadth, or a breadth suitable to their length;*
> *in a word, when everything has a symmetrical correspondence. . . . As*
> *in the human body, from cubit, foot, palm, inch and other small parts*
> *comes the symmetric quality of* **eurythmia**; *so it is in the completed*
> *building.*[88]

And, Vitruvius continues, the small part that guarantees *eurythmia* in a boat is given by the space between its rowlocks. Interestingly enough, in Book VI, his chapter on proportion in building once more makes mention of oars.[89] This is perhaps coincidental, or perhaps not. With the complete disappearance of Vitruvius' Greek sources, which he no doubt misunderstood and almost certainly romanized, there is no way of knowing.

The most straightforward derivation of the word *eurythmia* is from *eu*, good, well, and *rhythmos*, which is not only any regularly recurring motion (rhythm), but also shape or pattern. According to J. J. Pollitt, *rhythmoi*, in the terms used by classical Greek sculptors, were "patterns isolated within continual movement," and "a single well-chosen *rhythmos* could, in fact, convey the whole nature of movement."[90] Pollitt cites Myron's Discobolos as a particularly good example. With the terms taken at this level, the embodiment of the right *rhythmos* in a work of architecture in a way that perfectly attunes or adjusts it to its surrounding element is very much what *eurythmia* seems to have been all about.

Euērēs, an adjective used in Homer exclusively as a fixed epithet for oar (*eretmon*), means well-fitted: *eu*, well, *arērōs*, fitted together. Now why does Homer always refer to oars as well-fitted?[91] The first reason is fairly obvious. Oars must be well-fitted because the whole construction of a boat is a question of proper fitting. Oars must also, as Vitruvius notes, be evenly spaced in a bank of oars, for the dimension of the spaces between the rowlocks determines the well-fittedness of the entire vessel. Oars, to be well-fitted, must have the right shape: slightly curved, and flattened out at the bottom, where they are wider than at the top. If they are not flat and wide at the bottom they will not slice into the water to establish the right "fit" that is, paradoxically, the resistance or tension necessary to propel the boat forward. If oars are not narrow and round at the top, they will not fit the hand of the oarsmen properly and be useless for rowing, which is the right rhythm of oars beating the water in unison: what makes a boat "fly." Well-fitted oars, *euēre' eretma*, are the perfect attunement of a boat to its surrounding element, and I would contend that in the very concrete thinking of the builders of the first peripteral temples, *eurythmia*, whatever else it was, was also *euēre' eretma*.

Setting Up Looms

As essential a constituent of the Greek household (*oikos*) as its hearth (*hestia*) was its loom (*histon*). The extremely time-consuming process of hand weaving[92] makes the loom an emblem of the *oikos*'s stability as well as of its self-sufficiency, just as is Penelope's loom in the *Odyssey*. At night, Penelope undoes the work done during the day to win time from her

Women weaving on an upright, warp-weighted loom.

Greek lekythos, ca. 560 B.C.

unscrupulous suitors and preserve the integrity of her household against their persistent onslaughts. In fact, one might say that if Odysseus still had an **oikos** to come home to when he returned to Ithaca after twenty years' absence, it was largely thanks to Penelope's loom.

Ancient Greek looms were "set up" (**stēsasthai**).[93] They consisted of two upright posts (**histopodes**, loom feet) planted in the ground or in a floor equipped with post holes specific to the purpose. On top of these posts was placed the top or warp beam, from which the warp threads were hung, weighted by stone or ceramic warp weights which kept the threads taut.[94] The fabric was woven from the top down. These looms could, generally speaking, be dismantled for storage when not in use.

Archaeological evidence shows that upright warp-weighted looms were in use in the Aegean area as early as the mid-third millennium B.C.[95] Now such looms were not exclusive to the Hellenic world. They appear in central and northern Europe and in Italy even earlier than in bronze age Greece. But, as I have been insisting, the Greeks of the archaic period understood craft as having a special, public role. Craftsmen were **dēmiourgoi**. People wove their cities to make them visible. The goddess of weaving was the goddess of the city.

Every household had a loom—had had one since the age of heroes. If one of the first things a Greek child saw, when he began to see at all, was his mother, one of the very next things he saw would almost certainly have been the loom at which his mother worked. Weaving, it has been remarked, is one of the few activities compatible with simultaneous child-watching.[96] Mothers, weaving, watched their children. Small children watched their mothers ceaselessly weaving on upright looms that must, to them, have seemed monumental, as big as houses. Looms and houses: for the Greeks, the loom and the household of which it was such an integral feature must have shared something of the same identity. And as we know, only householders (by definition, loom owners) could be citizens of the *polis*.

One of the first tasks of an *oikistēs*, oikist—colonizer, city founder—when he arrived at the site of a new city was to establish the public hearth of the new foundation, lit with sacred fire transported from the *metropolis*.[97] The root of the word *oikistēs* is, of course, *oikos*, and the symbolism of bringing sacred fire to a public hearth in the *agora* of a new city could not speak more clearly of the oikists' intention to give their foundations the stability of home or dwelling place. But surely if, as I have argued, hearth (*hestia/histia*)[98] and loom (*histon*) are bound not only etymologically by the notion of setting up, or making fixed (*histēmi*), but also by their shared constitutive role in the Greek household, it is not unreasonable to expect the oikists, when setting up new households abroad, to have equipped these not only with hearths but also with looms.

The vertical, warp-weighted loom is about the simplest example imaginable of post-and-beam or trabeated structure. For the Greeks, it was certainly the most familiar one. The structure was not significant in itself. That it had been, since time immemorial, the structure of a loom, made it so.

Structurally, the *pteron* of a peripteral temple is all post-and-beam. Indeed, one of the first things the beginning student of architectural history learns is that whereas the Romans invented arches, the Greeks celebrated trabeation, and this, as far as it goes, is perfectly true. But the Greeks were not celebrating a structural *system*. Notions of structural systems, as such, would have been completely foreign to them. The Greeks, when they built the temples without which the *polis* could not come to be, were setting up looms. Certainly, as the commentators have noted, the *ptera*, at least the first ones, could not have been meant as sheltering porches: they were not deep enough. Nor did the *pteron* have any structural role, except to support the roof extended to cover it; eaves which, if one dismisses the notion of protecting the *naos* walls, had no function either, except, like sheltering wings, to protect the *pteron*, which was primary. A little lamely, the commentators conclude that the *pteron* was intended for display. For displaying what? For displaying trabeation? I would say for making visible the loom, or looms, that wove the city. Post-and-beam soon became column and entablature; it was elaborated to include base, capital, architrave, frieze, cornice. These parts were in turn elaborated. *Kosmos* increases visibility. The basic unit, the frame, remained that of a vertical warp-weighted loom, which consisted of two posts and a beam.

A *pteron*, in its structural essentials, is constituted as a linked sequence of such frames, where the posts of one frame support not only their own beam but also one end of each of the two beams extending over the frames on either side. Remove one column, two looms collapse; remove a whole frame, and three looms no longer stand. The *pteron* ceases to be continuous. The upright looms of a temple *pteron* were not independent, like the autonomous looms of private households. Nor, like household looms, could they be dismantled for storage when they were not in use. They were always in use. Weaving the visible city was a perennial undertaking.[99]

It has been argued that seventh-century Greek monumental architecture, trabeation in particular, was Egyptian in

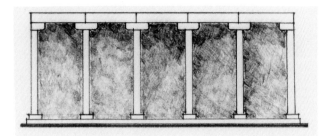

*The structural essentials of a temple **pteron.***

origin.[100] This may very well be so, for the Greeks did indeed understand the Egyptians to be the possessors of ancient wisdom of many kinds. But the Greeks never built pyramids, and Egyptian monuments, although they had many posts and beams, had no peristyles—no wings.

The trabeated structure, for the Egyptians, could have had no connection with weaving either, since Egyptians wove on horizontal ground looms,[101] not upright ones. The Egyptians, moreover, had no *dēmiourgoi*, no *poleis*. In Greece, the trabeated peristyle, whether of Egyptian inspiration or not, had a particularly Greek meaning.

To behold, with wonder, a Greek temple is first and foremost to become aware of its *pteron*. In fact the *pteron* is often the only thing still left standing. Its visibility, the visibility of a shrine set on a *topos* with *epiphaneia*, is also the visible interdependence of householder-citizens who together wove the emerging archaic Greek *polis*.

The anthropology that opens Book II of Vitruvius' *De Architectura*, one of many similar accounts for which the fifth-century atomist Democritus is considered to be the common

EX PRIMA MVNDI HOMINVM AETATE AEDIFICATIO · MVLTI ENIM AB ANIMALIBVS EXEMPLA VITAE CONSERVANÆ Q̃ IMITATI SVNT & C̃ᴬ

The first builders wove their walls.

source,[102] is Greek in origin. People, says Vitruvius, were first drawn together by fire, then by shared speech. It is difficult not to see in this account a reflection of how, in fact, Greek political communities first took shape around a sacred fire which burned in a public hearth set up in the ***agora***: the place where people assembled to ***agoreuein***—to speak to one another. The building of peripteral temples was also integral to the formation of the ***polis***. In Vitruvius' anthropology, community is consolidated when people begin to build: "And first, with upright forked props and twigs put between, they wove their walls."[103] Vitruvius' first structure is that of an upright Greek loom.

In the fifth century B.C. Pericles fixed the ritual of the Panathenaea into the form discussed earlier, and so distilled the
memory of emerging political order into a representation as
beautiful, as dynamic, and as revealing as the Parthenon frieze
that describes it. The same kind of distillation or refinement
occurred in the Parthenon itself and, to a certain extent, in
the other Periclean structures of the Athenian Acropolis.

Refinements did not, of course, originate with the Parthenon. Several temples had them, and some, such as the
Temple of Zeus at Olympia, predate the Parthenon. But the
refinements of the Parthenon are certainly the most "refined"
and the best known, having been the subject of study for nearly
two centuries:[104] the curved stylobate and entablature, the
slightly enlarged corner columns, the entasis of the columns,
which by then had become considerably less pronounced (more
"refined"—less like oars, in fact) than on earlier temples, and
so on. In a word, everything that might be expected to be
straight, perpendicular, or strictly level is built as curved or
slightly skewed. According to most interpretations, this was
done so that the perpendicular, the straight, and the horizontal
might indeed appear to be so, for the judgment of the eye
being inaccurate, as Vitruvius says,[105] "what is real seems
false"[106] and needs correcting in order to seem true.

Vitruvius' theory of optical corrections would appear to
originate in optical theories, notably that of Euclid,[107] which
were formulated considerably later than the building of the
Parthenon. Ictinus, too, may have had a theory of optics, but
if he did, which is unfortunately impossible to determine, the
Parthenon's refinements were not necessarily the application

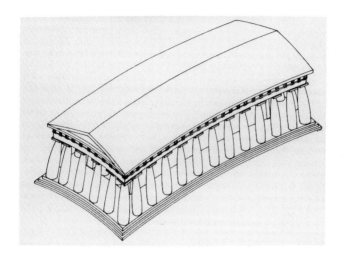

Doric temple showing exaggerated refinements.

of such a theory. The theory could very well have been a legitimation of the refinements. Perhaps the actual building of the refinements, rather than being the application of an optical theory, had more to do with concentrating in a single building all that Hellas knew, but could not articulate, about Daedalus' discovery of order, and about revealing, through the fixity of a single well-chosen ***rhythmos***, "the whole nature of movement," as Pollitt has put it.

We must therefore first determine the method of the symmetries from which these modifications [i.e., "optical corrections"] are to be correctly deduced. Then the unit of length for the site of the future work is to be set forth. When the magnitude of this is once determined, there will follow upon it the adjustment of the proportions to the decor [ad decorum] so that the appearance of eurythmy may be convincing to the observer [my emphasis].[108]

The Parthenon, Vincent Scully has remarked, "seems to be taking wing, . . . lifting and soaring despite its weight, the stones themselves rising. . . . The ptera now become true wings."[109] Wings, I would say, in the sense that Hesiod used *ptera*[110] when he spoke of boats and navigation. If the Parthenon does indeed seem about to take wing (or set sail) it does so because of the so-called refinements. These, when exaggerated as illustrated here, reveal all the tension—a tension which is itself neither movement nor fixity—of a bent bow about to release a winged arrow, or of the sail of a ship straining and swollen with the wind. When we view the Parthenon we do not see what the figure shows. The extreme subtlety of the refinements as built makes this impossible. But I strongly suspect that the intention of their building was to describe the tension not so much of arrested movement as of movement that is not yet, just as Myron's Discobolos does.

Phidias' colossal statue of Athena, which was housed in the Parthenon, held in its right hand a statue of Winged Victory, according to Pausanias,[111] about four cubits high. Shortly after Pericles' death in the plague of 429 B.C., there was completed on the spur of rock at the southwest extremity of the Acropolis the exquisite Ionic temple of Athena Nike, or Nike Apteros, Wingless Victory. The winglessness of Nike Apteros is of the same nature as the chains that bind a *xoanon*:[112] a revelation, for the Greeks, far more immediate than any winged representation, of a divine and animated presence. Indeed the small amphiprostyle temple, itself wingless and bound to its rock, seems, at least to this observer, even more likely to soar than the Parthenon.

It has been argued that the curvatures of the Parthenon were not intended to confer the impression of upward move-

Temple of Nike Apteros, 427 B.C.,
Acropolis, Athens.

ment, but rather the opposite. They were meant to anchor the temple firmly to the ground, to convince the viewer of its stability.[113] Of course they were: just like the chains that bound a statue, or Victory's sheared-off wings.

Ship, City, Temple

As discussed earlier, Jean-Pierre Vernant, in *The Origins of Greek Thought*, claims that the origin of the new image of the world embodied in Anaximander's cosmology is to be found in the emerging political order of archaic Greece. Crucial in this new image was the supremacy of the law of equilibrium, whereby "*monarchia* was replaced in nature, as in the city, by the rule of *isonomia*."[114] This idea formed a common ground for the thought of all the pre-Socratics, as well as for the medical theory of the early fifth century B.C., health being an *isonomia* or balance of powers, and sickness the *monarchia* of one element over another.

Bound up with the new importance of equilibrium was, according to Vernant, a new conception of space whereby power was located *en meson*, in the center: physically, in the city, in the *hestia koine*, the public hearth in the agora. For as Maeandrius, successor to the mid-sixth-century Samian tyrant Polycrates, is reported to have said, "I never approved . . . of Polycrates' reigning as a despot over men who were his equals. . . . For myself, I lay down the *archē en meson*, and I proclaim *isonomia* for you."[115] I do not wish to lay too much stress on the fact that this proclamation was made in Samos. What is important is that when, at Samos as elsewhere, the columns of the temple came outside, the power, the *archē* that was *en meson* in the *naos* with its cult statue and hearth place, was made to be seen to be located in the center. It has, admittedly, not been common to suggest a connection between peripteral columns and oars or, for that matter, between trabeated peristyles and looms,[116] but every architectural theoretician from Vitruvius until the eighteenth century has stressed the connection between columns and *people*: people, I would claim, who were assembled to stand in **isonomia** around the power located **en meson**, when the columns came to stand, equally spaced, around the **naos** of the first peripteral temples.

Craft brought people out of the isolation and barbarism personified by the cave-dwelling Cyclopes who had no assemblies or knowledge of boat building. Craft and community were, for the early Greeks, indissociable, and it was the peripteral temple, whose canon of construction became, over the years, almost invariable, that enshrined the memory of this conviction. The sacrifices which had affirmed community and propitiated the gods before the time of temples and had taken place around altars whose location had become fixed by tradition were now, for the most part, linked directly with the presence of a temple building that was, with its **pteron** of equally spaced columns, itself a reaffirmation of the meaning of the sacrifice. The **kosmos** of the **pteron**, its order and its ornament, consisting as it eventually did, according to George Hersey, of parts whose names were also those of the parts of sacrificial victims, could not have made this more evident.

In the building of the temple was concentrated both the making and the discovery of **kosmos**, which, at least from Hesiod onward, was explicitly understood as the province of the divine. Thus, the temple not only became the location for the embodiment of the indissociability of craft and community, but also replaced the caves and sacred groves of earlier divine epiphanies, to become the place where the presence of the god or goddess was revealed.

There is nothing in this that is at odds with the notion of the peripteral temple as a ship, or with viewing its **pteron** as a linked series of looms that bodied forth the political interdependence of households. On the contrary. Oars are set in motion by oarsmen equally spaced, like their oars, around the ship's periphery, and it is only when the oarsmen ply these oars *together*, keeping time to a rhythm that is of no single man's making, that the boat can properly take flight.

"It is men that make a **polis**," said Nicias to his soldiers on the beach at Syracuse, "not walls or ships devoid of men."[117]

Early protoattic krater, ca. 710–700 B.C.

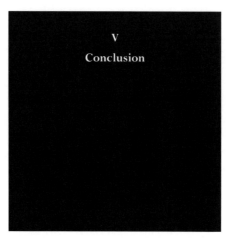

V

Conclusion

*For the same reason we consider that the master craftsmen [**architek-tonas**] in every profession are more estimable and know more and are wiser than the artisans [**cheirotechnōn**—literally, hand-workers] because they know the reasons of the things which are done.*[1]

The several arts are composed of two things—craftsmanship and the theory of it [ex opere et eius rationatione]. Of these the one, craftsmanship, is proper to those who are trained in the several arts, namely the execution of the work; the other, namely theory, is shared with educated persons. . . . Throughout all the sciences many things, or indeed all, are in common so far as theory is concerned. But the taking up of work which is finely executed by hand, or technical methods, belongs to those who have been specially trained in a single trade.[2]

The consensus among scholars is that Anaximander's treatise, claimed to be at once the West's first work in prose and its first work of philosophy, appeared around the beginning of the second half of the sixth century B.C. But if Vitruvius is to be believed, at the same time Rhoikos and Theodorus published a work, also presumably (although not necessarily) in prose, on "the Ionic temple of Juno which is at Samos":[3] the first architectural treatise.

Anaximander's work has become, in the history of philosophy, the first recorded articulation of Western thought, with his cosmic model, the built work, all but forgotten and treated by historians as, at best, somewhat incidental. Nothing remains of the "Ionic temple of Juno" Rhoikos and Theodorus built. It burned down in 530 B.C. and was replaced shortly afterward by the fourth Samian Heraion, the largest of all Greek temples. Of this only a single, precarious stack of column

Ruins of the temple of Hera at Samos.

drums remains, surrounded by a litter of bases and broken stones. Rhoikos' and Theodorus' written work has all but been forgotten, and would no doubt have been so entirely had it not been for Vitruvius' mention of it.

Anaximander's work, and with it the dawn of Western thought, cannot be understood apart from the craft which was, for the early Greeks, the appearing of **kosmos**. Anaximander's work, in other words, cannot be understood apart from his model, and this is why I have tried, even in the face of very scanty evidence, to imagine what that model may have been like. The attempt to envision the model has led to the conclusion that what is known of Anaximander's cosmology, together with the thought expressed in the B1 fragment, can be understood as a theory of the work, just as Vitruvius understood the treatise of Rhoikos and Theodorus to be the theory of the temple of Hera at Samos.

Vitruvius calls the written work in which the theory of the built one is articulated a *commentarius*, a commentary, from the verb *commentor*, think over. In Book I, where he discusses the range of knowledge an architect should possess, he says that an architect ought to know letters, "so that he may achieve a stronger memory in commentaries [*uti commentariis memoriam firmiorem efficere possit*]."[4] If, in a commentary, an architect "thinks over" his built work and, through writing, commits it to memory, then obviously the built work must come first.

The peripteral temple, and the emerging *polis* of whose making the temple was both an essential constituent and an emblem, did not appear *with* the birth of theory. Their appearing took place over the two-hundred-year period that *preceded* it. It is crucial to understand the significance of this chronology, the relevance of this "order of time."

Theōria had, originally, to do both with seeing and with the revelation of the divine, which converged, in Homeric literature, in the wondering admiration, the *thauma*, with which Homeric eyes beheld the well-made things that were *daidala*: things animated with a divine life that revealed the hidden presence of a goddess or a god. "It is through wonder [*to thaumazein*] that men now begin and originally began to philosophize," says Aristotle in a celebrated passage near the beginning of the *Metaphysics*.[5] But before there could be wonder (or theory, or philosophy, or architectural treatises), there had to be the well-made thing.

And this is where the difficulty arises, a difficulty that lies at the very root of what Heidegger has lamented as the objectivization of Being in Western metaphysics. *Kosmos* is discovered, as Daedalus discovered it, through a *technē* that is a letting appear. Homeric *epistēmē*, like Homeric *sophia*,[6] had to do with skill: knowledge or wisdom that could not be separated from the experience of the knower. The feet of the dancers in Ariadne's dance are *epistamenoisi*,[7] knowing feet, and one cannot claim to have knowledge of dancing until one can, in fact, dance. Icarus, in the legend, lacked his father's *sophia* and drowned because he did. Theory, on the other hand, demands that the well-made thing *already be made*, that it have already appeared: *eidos*, the thing seen, an object of knowledge in whose being the knower no longer participates with his own.

The experiential dimension of *sophia* as skill continued to be recognized in the classical period, for Socrates is quoted as speaking of the *sophia* of Daedalus, both in the passage from the *Euthyphro* cited in the introduction to this essay as well as in one from Xenophon's *Memorabilia*.[8] But Socrates finds the *sophia* of his ancestor, at best, a little ridiculous. By the second century A.D., Plutarch feels the need to explain what this kind of *sophia* *is*, so at odds is it with what, by then, has become known as wisdom. Speaking of Mnesiphilus, Themistocles' mentor, Plutarch calls him "a man who was neither a rhetorician nor one of the so-called physical philosophers, but a cultivator of what was then called *sophia*, although it was really nothing more than cleverness in politics and practical sagacity."[9]

For Plato, *epistēmē* and *sophia* no longer had anything to do with skill. Daedalean *epistēmē*, the uncertain, elusive knowledge of experience, was subsumed to, absorbed by, the certainty of knowledge as seeing, *eidenai*, with the *eidos*, the thing seen, fixed and eternal, as its ultimate object and source. And although the experiential dimension of wisdom continued to linger in the classical understanding of it, no one, according to Plato, could claim to be truly *sophos*, only to be *philo-sophos*, a lover of wisdom. True wisdom was exclusively the province of the divine, and beyond the reach of human experience. The earlier understanding that *sophia*-as-skill, the complement of a *technē* that allowed *kosmos* to appear,[10] was itself the very revelation of the divine in experience, had been lost. But if, according to Plato, people cannot experience *sophia*, how can they know what it is, or recognize it as divine, so that they may come to love it? Where does *epistēmē* come from, if it is not living knowledge, knowledge-as-skill?

From memory. *Epistēmē*, according to Plato, is true opinion (*doxa*) bound by the chains of recollection (*anamnēsis*). For Plato, this recollection is the memory of the world of Ideas (*eidē*) known before birth.

Which birth? Whose? Was it the birth of bright-eyed Athena who, in that "outrageous myth . . . a diagram of motherless birth,"[11] sprang fully armed from the head of Zeus, never having known the darkness of the womb? The unnatural birth the Athenians exalted on the east pediment of the Parthenon?[12] The birth whose sculptural glorification virtually eclipsed the panathenaic frieze, and its celebration of the *peplos*, which was all but hidden near the top of the *naos* walls inside the *pteron*?

The men of classical Greece, especially the men of Athens, for whom Aeschylus spoke when he said "The mother is no parent of her child,"[13] knew nothing about birth.

Plato's theory of recollection assumed that knowledge of the ideal was perfect and complete before birth. If this theory is considered in the context of the rather offensive classical Greek view of the facts of life, and if one recalls that the womb is symbolized by the cave of the *Republic* as the location of brute ignorance, then Plato, one is inevitably led to conclude, must have assumed the ideal state of perfect knowledge to have existed before conception, in the pristine state of uncontaminated, no doubt luminous, male seed.

There is, however, nothing objectionable in the theory of recollection itself or in the notion of knowledge as the recall in life of a world known before birth, if this world is rightly understood as the world of experience known before there is any objective seeing. The seeing person cannot, of course, forget that he or she sees, and any recollection of the pre-seeing state is necessarily made in terms of seeing, for there is no return to the womb.

The memory of a pre-seeing, pretheoretical world of letting appear, the memory of a world where *epistēmē* and *sophia* both were skill, was lost, along with the memory of Being, in Western metaphysics. But, if my speculations regarding Anaximander's work have any validity, metaphysics itself emerged from that very kind of *epistēmē*,[14] and for the brief pre-Socratic period the two kinds of *epistēmē*, the skillful kind and the seeing kind, coexisted in a tenuous balance in Western thought. By the fifth century, perhaps as a result of the Persian conquest of Ionia and of the hegemony of Athens, the balance tipped irrevocably in favor of seeing.

However, if the memory of the pre-seeing world was lost in Western metaphysics, it was, I would claim, preserved in Western architecture, and in its theory, which shared the identity of metaphysics for that brief time in the sixth century B.C. If Vitruvius and his successors are read with patience, the traces of this concurrence can still be found. It becomes clear, for example, why the legitimacy of the Doric order was claimed to have rested on its resemblance to carpentry. The importance was not to preserve the memory of wood construction as such, but, with the building of each Doric temple, to bind with the chains of recollection into an *epistēmē* as seeing the *doxa*, the right opinion, that cutting, assembly, and the perfect adjustment of parts were essential in the realm of *epistēmē* as skill in allowing *kosmos* to appear. When read in the light of the early Greek understanding of craft and *epiphaneia*, Alberti's insistence that the temple be built in a "proud place" and be "perfectly visible from every direction"[15] is a similar recollection of how *kosmos* appears through *technē*. Likewise, in the architectural theory of sixteenth-century France, seeing and pre-seeing wisdom converge in the *sapience* of Philibert de l'Orme's *sage et docte architecte*, whose *sophia* is at once Daedalean and Socratic, experiential and theoretic.

Kosmos was, as we have seen, also political, with the making of the *polis* and its emblem, the temple, the very embodiment of the building and navigation of a boat, the weaving of a cloth, or the tracing of the figure of a dance. Socrates no longer understood or appreciated the role the artifact played as the sensible vehicle and anchor for political *kosmos*. But the vocabulary he uses in speaking of civic harmony betrays its hidden source:

*And wise men tell us, Callicles, that heaven and earth and gods and men are held together by communion and friendship, by orderliness, temperance and justice; and that is the reason, my friend, why they call the whole of this world by the name of **kosmos**.*[16]

For Socrates, political *kosmos* is part of a cosmic order, held together by harmonious relationships such as sharing and friendship. This is classical theory, voiced in abstract terms. But in preclassical Greece, *harmonia*, and its manifestation in political **kosmos**, were still part of a cosmos understood concretely, through artifacts that held together because of their flawless, perfectly adjusted joints. The archaic world was a world that appeared through the things people made. The **polis** and the well-built temples that made it appear shared a common identity. Craft and community were indissoluble.

When, in the classical period, **epistēmē** became seeing, not only did the craftsman lose his prestige and become divorced from the political sphere, but so did the thinker, the **philo-sophos**. Indeed, for all his eloquence on the matter of civic harmony, Socrates met his death, in part at least, because he lacked political commitment.

It is fairly common today among certain enlightened architectural historians to claim that architecture, until the eighteenth century, was built metaphysics. My claim is that not only metaphysics but all of Western thinking was first grounded in architecture, and that, until the eighteenth century, the legitimacy of architecture rested on the preservation of that memory.

Notes

Introduction: Socrates' Ancestor

1. Plato *Euthyphro* 11c–e. The Jowett translation renders the **sophia** of Daedalus as his "wisdom." The earliest usages of **sophia**, in Homer, Herodotus, and even later, had to do, specifically, with skill in craft—especially in carpentry, but also in other crafts. If Daedalus was wise, he was so in this specific sense.

2. On Daedalus, see Frontisi-Ducroux 1975, Pérez-Gómez 1985, and especially Sarah P. Morris's recent, wide-ranging study (1992).

3. *Iliad* 18.590.

4. Diogenes Laertius 2.18. Diogenes also uses the word **lithoxoos**, stone or marble mason. The tenth-century lexicographer Suda (s.v. Socrates) calls Sophroniskos a **lithogluphos**, sculptor. Cf. Morris 1992, p. 258. Socrates' mother, Phalarete, was a midwife.

5. See also Plato *Alcibiades* 121a.

6. Morris (1992, p. 217) points out that Daedalus in the classical period almost always appears as a figure of fun: "A major proportion of classical references to Daidalos and his art are humorous, whether in comedies and satyr plays or in philosophy."

7. Reductive qualifiers like "nothing but" or "merely" appear on almost every other page of Cornford's *From Religion to Philosophy*. For example (Cornford 1957, p. 25) the river Styx is *"nothing but* the recoil or negative aspect of power. . . . [Styx] *is only* another form of Moira," and (p. 36) "The personal God of religion and the impersonal Reason of philosophy *merely* reenact as 'dispensers' . . . that old arrangement called Moira." Moira, in turn (p. 54), "is *simply* a projection, or extension of Nomos [law] from tribal group to the elemental grouping of the cosmos." If I seem to be flogging a long-dead horse (*From Religion to Philosophy* was, after all, first published in 1912), I would point out that more recently the German classicist Walter Burkert has adopted tactics of a similar nature. As the

French anthropologist Jean-Louis Durand has remarked, "on ne sort pas du frazérisme" (Durand 1986, p. 4).

8.   Although Eric Voegelin has condemned Heidegger as "that ingenious gnostic of our own time" (Voegelin 1968, p. 46), I would claim that, Voegelin's theological bent apart, the concern with emergence (in Voegelin, history as emerging consciousness: volumes 4 and 5 of *Order* and *History* especially; in Heidegger, Being as revealed through emergence in the thought of the pre-Socratics) links the two thinkers at a very fundamental level.

9.   That architecture is an embodiment of ritual has been argued, among others, by Joseph Rykwert, Alberto Pérez-Gómez, and, insofar as he demonstrates the constituent parts of Greek temples to be named for the parts of sacrificial victims, by George Hersey.

10. Plato *Hippias Major* 282a.

11. Plato *Meno* 97d–98a.

12. Frontisi-Ducroux 1975, pp. 103ff. The cult statue of Hera at Samos, for example, was a crudely carved wooden *xoanon* which was chained except on feast days, when it was "freed" to move about in sacred processions. Before taking the form of a *xoanon*, the cult image of Hera had been simply a plank (*sanis*). Sarah P. Morris claims that the association between Daedalus and *xoana*, and indeed the allegation that Daedalus was first, before he was anything else, an Athenian sculptor, was an Athenian fabrication and a product of classical Athenian chauvinism, born with Athens' defeat of the Persians at Salamis in 480 B.C. On *xoana* see also A. A. Donohue's exhaustive study (1988).

13. Plato *Meno* 98a.

———————————————— II ————————————————

Anaximander and the Articulation of Order

1. His dates, which are usually given as 610 to 546 B.C., with a *floruit* of about 560, coincide with the last years of Ionian colonization. Miletus itself was referred to as "the mother of colonies."

2. In the classical period, Thales was numbered among the so-called seven sages (*sophoi*) of archaic Greece, along with his contemporaries Solon the legislator and Epimenides the prophet.

3. Herodotus 1.75.

4. Herodotus 1.170.

5. Simplicius (commentary on *Physics*; Diels 1952, pp. 23, 29) says that Thales "is said to have left nothing in the form of writings except the so-called 'Nautical Star Guide,'" whereas according to Diogenes Laertius (1.23), "he left no book behind; for the 'Nautical Star Guide' ascribed to him is said to be by Phokos, the Samian." Cf. Kirk, Raven, and Schofield 1983, p. 86. Although the authorship of the "Nautical Star Guide" must, in the light of conflicting evidence, be considered dubious, generally speaking Simplicius, who has been argued to have had in hand Theophrastus' **Physikōn doxai** as a source, is considered more reliable than Diogenes Laertius. Whether by Thales or not, the "Nautical Star Guide" did not survive, and even the earliest commentators seem not to have seen it.

6. By the Diels (1952) numbering, direct quotations are numbered "B" and indirect comments or elucidations numbered "A."

7. Kahn 1960, p. 166.

8. Vlastos 1947, p. 170.

9. Ibid.

10. Vlastos 1952, p. 54.

11. Hesiod *Theogony* 116ff.

12. See, among others, Jaeger 1947, p. 13, and Kirk, Raven, and Schofield 1983, p. 39.

13. Aristotle *Physics* 203b6 (**periechein apanta kai panta kubernan**). The verb **kubernaō** is primarily a navigational term, meaning to steer, or to act as helmsman. The phrase, though Aristotle's, is considered to have very much the character of a direct quote: see Jaeger 1947, p. 30.

14. **Kosmos** in prephilosophical Greece was order of any kind. It only becomes world order or universal order after Anaximander, whose cosmology is the turning point.

15. **Tois ousi: ta onta** appears in the dative, not the genitive case.

16. **Hetera tis physis apeiros**: the indefinite article **tis** (some), together with qualifier **hetera** (different or other), suggests that the **physis** referred to is not only boundless (**apeiros**) but essentially unknown and unnamable. The objectified **to apeiron**, *the* Boundless, does not appear inside the direct quotation from Anaximander, and it is likely that Anaximander did not even use the qualifier as a substantive. For him **apeiros** was a quality of an unnamable **physis**.

    Use of the word **physis** is not attested for "nature-as-coming-to-be" until Heraclitus in the very late sixth century, some time after Anaximander. The word does occur once in Homer (*Odyssey* 10.303), however, where Hermes shows Odysseus the **physis** of the moly plant by showing him its black root and white flower. The moly's **physis**, insofar as Hermes demonstrates it to consist of both root and blossom, can be understood to mean the plant's coming-to-be, its coming-to-light (from **phuō**, emerge, come to light), in essentially the same sense as the Heraclitean sense of **physis**, which can also, therefore, justifiably be taken as Anaximander's sense.

17. "The Anaximander Fragment," in Heidegger 1984, p. 54.

18. *Iliad* 2.214, 8.12, 10.472, 11.48, etc.; *Odyssey* 3.138, 8.179, 489, 492, 14.363, etc.

19. As a neuter plural demonstrative pronoun *tauta* cannot simply refer to *kosmoi*, which is masculine. "The foregoing things," which include *kosmoi*, *ouranoi*, and ultimately *tis physis apeiros*, seems to me to be the reading most consistent with taking *kosmoi* as the referent for *hōn*.

20. ". . . *to chreōn* is the oldest name in which thinking brings the Being of beings to language" (Heidegger 1984, p. 49).

21. Ibid., p. 29.

22. "Why did I cease before I gained the objects for whose sake I brought together the people? The great mother of the Olympian deities would be my best supporting witness for this in the court of Time [*en dikēi Chronou*]." Solon fr. 24, cited on p. 121 of Kirk, Raven, and Schofield (1983), who also stress the similarity to the assessment of time in the Anaximander fragment.

23. Homer uses *chronos* when he speaks of a while, as in a long while or a short while. For example, Odysseus addressing the assembly of Achaeans in the *Iliad* says "Endure, my friends, and abide for a time [*epi chronon*]" (*Iliad* 2.299), and in the *Odyssey* Telemachus says to Menelaus, "Son of Atreus, keep me no long time [*polyn chronon*] here" (*Odyssey* 4.594). In Homer, *chronos* is *durée*. With Herodotus, the first historian, *chronos* emerges as chronology (ordered *durée*), as for example when he discusses the development of Greek mythology:
    Then after a long while [*de chronou pollou*] *they learned the names of the rest of the gods . . . and* presently [*meta chronon*] *they inquired of the oracle at Dodona concerning the names, for this place of divination is held to be the most ancient in Hellas, and* at that time [*ēn ton chronon*] *it was the only one. . . . From that time onwards [*apo men dē toutou tou chronou*] they used the names of the gods in their sacrifices.* (Herodotus 2.52)
    Anaximander is (chronologically) halfway between Homer and Herodotus.

24. It is worth noting the distinction Aristotle makes between *aiōn* and *chronos* in *On the Heavens* (279a2off). *Aiōn* (from *aei*, always, and

ōn, being) is characterized as a circle; complete, with no beginning and no end, and Aristotle says, "this word *aiōn* possessed a divine significance for the ancients; for the fulfilment [*telos*] which encompasses [*periechon*] the time [*chronos*] of each life . . . has been called its *aiōn*."

25. Aristotle *Physics* 203b6. See note 13, above.

26. *Apeiros*, in Homer, is a qualifier of earth and sea, but chiefly of the earth, and these in epic poetry are not thought *except* as qualified, by this or other qualifiers. As a qualifier—a feature of experience—*apeiros*, whose gender, as an adjective, changed with the gender of the thing qualified, acquired independent ontological status by the addition of the definite article *to*, whereby its gender also became fixed as neuter. There is no evidence that Anaximander ever, himself, neutralized *apeiros*, since *to apeiron* only appears in the commentaries, and not in the verbatim quotation. It is significant that even much later, when Aristotle distinguishes between things that exist for themselves (*kath' hauta*) and those that exist attributively (*kata symbebēkos*), he classifies *to apeiron* as something that exists attributively (*kata symbebēkos esti to apeiron*; *Physics* 204a15), which is to say qualitatively.

27. Vernant 1974, p. 250.

28. The Greek term for prose writer is *logopoios*: *logos*, word, reason, computation; *poieō*, I make. A *logopoios* is to be contrasted with a *mythopoios*, a fabulist, or composer of fiction. The implication is that the writing of prose has to do with the relating of fact, and that the adoption of prose as a medium of expression signaled an awareness of, and an importance attached to, the distinction between fact and fiction. Although there is no textual evidence that Anaximander was ever referred to as a *logopoios*, Herodotus refers twice (5.36, 125) to Anaximander's successor, the Milesian geographer/historian Hecataeus (fl. ca. 520 B.C.), as a *logopoios*.

29. This, of course, is only one dimension of the second fragment of Heraclitus, albeit an important one (cf. Kirk, Raven, and Schofield 1983, p. 187): "Therefore it is necessary to follow the common;

but although the **logos** is common [**xynos**, or **koinos** as it is rendered in Attic], many live as though they had a private understanding." **Logos**, whatever else it may be, is also speech: from **legō**, I speak.

30. **Epi tōn skiothērōn**—literally, upon the shadow-trackers. Cf. also Vitruvius 1.6.6.

31. Diogenes Laertius 2.1–2. Cf. Kirk, Raven, and Schofield 1983, p. 100. The translation is by Kirk, Raven, and Schofield.

32. Suda s.v. Anaximander; cf. Kirk, Raven, and Schofield 1983, p. 101, and Heidel 1921, p. 240.

33. Heidel 1921.

34. See Kahn 1960, pp. 75ff., Kirk, Raven, and Schofield 1983, pp. 103ff., and Vernant 1982, pp. 112ff. Herodotus 2.109: "The Greeks learned from the Babylonians of the celestial sphere and the *gnomon* and the twelve parts of the day."

35. Vernant 1982, p. 112.

36. Jean-Pierre Vernant's view (Vernant 1982) is that just as the Babylonians placed a hierarchical order in the heavens, so the Greeks, with the pre-Socratics, placed an incipient democratic order in the heavens. It is a view that, to a certain extent, obviates what I perceive as the pre-Socratic attempt to articulate reciprocity. The role of the emerging **polis** in Anaximander's cosmology may be undeniable, but it is not necessarily exclusive.

37. **Kionos lithos**—literally, the stone of a column. Hyppolytus 1.6.3.; cf. Kahn 1960, p. 55, and Kirk, Raven, and Schofield 1983, p. 133.

38. The birth of theory followed the advent of literacy in Greece in the eighth century B.C. Anne Carson's assessment of the significance of this departure is as illuminating as it is eloquent:
The inhabitants of an oral society live much more intimately blended with their surroundings than we do. . . . What is vital, in a world of sound, is to maintain continuity. . . . [But] a reader must disconnect himself from the

influx of sense-impressions transmitted by nose, ear, tongue and skin if he is to concentrate upon his reading. A written text separates words from one another, separates words from the environment, separates words from the reader (or writer) and separates the reader (or writer) from his environment. Separation is painful . . . written words project their user into isolation. (Carson 1986, pp. 49–50)

39. Cf. Rausch 1982, pp. 22ff.

40. Accents were not introduced in Greek until the third century B.C., and I suspect that their introduction had a great deal to do with an attempt to differentiate things that at an earlier stage were understood to be the same, or at least qualitatively similar.

41. See Bill 1901, p. 197; Rausch 1982, pp. 14ff.

42. *Theos*: god; *ōra*: care.

43. As for example in Theognis 805ff., a passage discussed at greater length below. See also Bill 1901, p. 196, and Rausch 1982, pp. 18ff.

44. Rausch 1982, p. 18.

45. See, for example, *Iliad* 7.444, where the gods "marvelled at [*thēeunto*] the great work of the bronze-coated Achaeans"—the wall the Achaeans built to shut off their ships from the Trojans—and *Odyssey* 2.13, where the people "marvelled at [*thēeunto*]" Telemachus as he entered the assembly because he was clothed in a "wondrous grace" shed upon him by the goddess Athena.

46. For example, "truly a great marvel is this that my eyes behold [*hē mega thauma tod' ophthalmoisin horōmai*]." *Iliad* 13.99, 15.286, 20.344, 21.54. Also, typically, "but at the sight they marvelled [*hoi de idontes thaumazon*] . . . [and] when they had satisfied their eyes with gazing [*horōmenoi ophthalmoisin*] . . . ." *Odyssey* 4.44–47.

47. *Iliad* 24.629.

48. *Odyssey* 24.370.

49. *Odyssey* 19.36.

50. *Iliad* 5.725.

51. *Iliad* 10.439.

52. *Iliad* 18.83.

53. *Iliad* 18.377.

54. *Odyssey* 7.45.

55. *Odyssey* 8.366.

56. *Odyssey* 13.108.

57. Hesiod *Theogony* 581.

58. Kirk, Raven, and Schofield (1983, p. 104) claim that its existence is improbable, first, because it is based on a single, unsubstantiated reference in Diogenes Laertius (2.2; see note 31 above), and second, because of the complexity of Anaximander's theory of the heavenly bodies. Kahn (1960, p. 89) assumes the existence of the sphere but supposes that, rather than a three-dimensional construction, it may simply have been a chart "of the sort used in ancient representations of the zodiac."

59. See Snodgrass 1967, ch. 3.

60. See Kahn 1960, pp. 85ff., and Kirk, Raven, and Schofield 1983, pp. 134–135.

61. Aëtius 2.20. Cf. Kirk, Raven, and Schofield 1983, p. 135.

62. In fact the English word "felloe" derives from the old Germanic *felhan*, which means to fit together (OED).

63. Archimedes (ca. 287–212 B.C.) is reported to have built a celestial globe that was mechanical. See Cicero *De republica* 1.14.

64. Vitruvius 9.1.2. The translation here is my own.

65. Agathemerus 1.1–2 as cited in Kahn 1960, p. 82; cf. Kirk, Raven, and Schofield 1983, p. 104.

66. Hyppolytus 1.6.3. Cf. Kirk, Raven, and Schofield 1983, pp. 133–134; these authors translate *epipedōn* as "*flat* surfaces," but an *epipedos* is simply a surface, not necessarily a flat one, which is important in view of the possibility, discussed below, that Anaximander's earth, or at least his map, had a convex surface.

67. Both Kahn (1960, p. 83) and Kirk, Raven, and Schofield (1983, p. 104) translate *eousan kukloterea hōs apo tornou* as "circular as if drawn with a compass." "Turned on a lathe" is an acceptable alternative reading, since a *tornos* can be a compass or a lathe.

68. Herodotus 4.36.

69. See Coulton 1977, p. 24, and Johannes 1937. Theodorus of Samos, who with his father Rhoikos was architect of the sixth-century Samian Heraion, is credited with having invented the lathe, or compass, or both, along with the square and the level.

70. *Odyssey* 1.141, 4.57, 16.49.

71. *Odyssey* 12.67.

72. *Enetetmēto*, a participle of the verb *entemnō* meaning cut or cut up, in contexts such as this one is usually translated as "engraved." However, since the verb is also used to refer to the cutting up of animals in sacrifice (apportioning of the victim), "engraved" as the description of how the map was made does not necessarily cover all the possibilities.

73. *Gēs apasēs periodos . . . kai thalassa te pasa kai potamoi pantes* (Herodotus 5.49).

74. Herodotus 5.49–50.

75. When Eric H. Warmington cites this passage he notes that "the map here dealt with was probably Anaximander's, if not Hecataeus's" (Warmington 1934, p. 229).

76. See Snodgrass 1967, pp. 53–54, and note 72 above.

77. The manuscript, apparently, has **ugron**, moist, which most interpreters change to **guron**, curved. Cf. Kahn 1960, p. 55; Kirk, Raven, and Schofield 1983, pp. 133–134.

78. Diels 1879, p. 218. Cf. Kahn 1960, p. 55; Kirk, Raven, and Schofield 1983, p. 133. Kahn suggests that the "curved" surface of the earth refers to its concavity: the concavity of the Mediterranean basin.

79. *Odyssey* 1.50.

80. *Iliad* 4.448, 6.118, 8.62, 11.259, etc.

81. See Snodgrass 1967, p. 53, and compare the illustration on p. 94 above.

82. *Iliad* 18.607–608.

83. *Iliad* 18.483.

84. Herodotus 1.29.

85. Some translators render **periodos** as circumference or outline. I think this is wrong. A **hodos** is a path, or a way, and a path, as anyone who has ever lived in the country knows, is traced by the passage of human feet. In Homer, especially in the *Odyssey*, **hodos** is traveling or journeying (2.285, 8.150, etc.). Later, a work of descriptive geography was called a **periploos**, a circumnavigation (a **ploion** is a ship), with the same evocation of traveling or movement.

86. **Thaumasthēnai to pragma**. See above.

87. The temporality of the shield is mentioned in Frontisi-Ducroux 1975, p. 74. As Frontisi-Ducroux further observes, although the

later, fifth-century B.C., pseudo-Hesiodic *Shield of Heracles* owes a great deal to its Homeric precedent, its structure becomes much more spatial than temporal.

Significantly, Homer's description of Achilles' shield is a dynamic description of its actual *making* by Hephaestus: "First fashioned he a shield . . . therein he wrought the earth . . . therein fashioned he also two cities of mortal men" and so on (*Iliad* 18.478ff.). The *Shield of Heracles*, whose composition is virtually contemporary with Anaximander's *floruit*, is a static description of the completed artifact: ". . . and a wonder it was to see [*thauma idesthai*] . . . in the centre was Fear . . . there were heads of snakes . . . on the shield stood the fleet-footed horses of grim Ares," etc. (140ff.). Cf. Hurwit 1985, p. 230. Hurwit observes that the technique of the author of the *Shield* "is the technique of a literate poet, one who fixes things on paper, not an oral poet, who creates as he performs."

88. Diogenes Laertius 2.1.

89. **Polos**: any kind of pivot, the axis of the celestial sphere, or, as Kirk, Raven, and Schofield have it (1983, p. 103), the celestial sphere itself.

90. Cf. Vitruvius 9.6.2.

91. *Iliad* 7.186–189.

92. *Odyssey* 2.159.

93. See, among others, Harrison 1912, p. 100.

94. *Odyssey* 13.311–313.

95. **Eidos** is the neuter perfect participle of **oida**: the thing that has been seen.

96. Aeschylus *Agamemnon* 1130. **Thesphatos**, literally, means spoken by a god: from **theos**, god, and **phēmi**, I speak or utter.

97. ". . . *mundique et astrorum*" (Vitruvius 2.1.2).

98. Theognis is the first to use **theōros** to mean an oracle questioner. Cf. Rausch 1982, pp. 18ff.

99. See also Heraclitus, fr. 93: "The lord whose oracle is in Delphi neither speaks out [*legei*] nor conceals [*kryptei*] but gives a sign [*sēmainei*]." Cf. Kirk, Raven, and Schofield 1983, p. 209.

100. Theognis 805ff. Cf. Rausch 1982, p. 18 and in note 24, p. 185.

101. See Heidel 1937, pp. 2ff.

102. Not until Plato (cf. *Phaedo* 97b–99d, 110b) does the shape of the earth become spherical to reflect the spherical configuration of the heavens. Cf. Heidel 1937, pp. 63ff.

103. See Vitruvius 9.6.1: "For from that revolution of the firmament and the contrary motion of the sun through the [zodiacal] signs and the equinoctial shadows of the gnomons, the diagrams of the analemma are discovered."

104. Plato *Timaeus* 38b–c.

III

Daedalus and the Discovery of Order

1. Plato *Timaeus* 38b.

2. As discussed earlier, Anaximander uses the indefinite article **tis**, some, to speak of "some" **apeiros physis**, some boundless nature that encompasses and steers (**kubernan**—the term, it must be recalled, is navigational) all things. Plato uses the definite article **hē** (the genitive of which, in the context cited, is **tēs**), to speak of *the* eternal nature on whose pattern the universe is modeled.

3. See Coulton 1977, pp. 55ff.

4. See P. Vidal-Naquet's introduction to Frontisi-Ducroux 1975, p. 12, and also Burford 1972.

5. Herodotus 2.167: "I know that in nearly all foreign countries those who learn trades . . . are held in less esteem than the rest of the people. . . . This opinion, which is held by all Greeks and chiefly by the Lacedaemonians, is of foreign origin." Cf. Burford 1972, p. 34.

6. See p. 159, "Building, Dwelling, Thinking," in Heidegger 1971: "The Greek for 'to bring forth or to produce' is *tikto*. The word *techne*, technique, belongs to the verb's root *tec*. To the Greeks *techne* means neither art nor handicraft but rather: to make something appear. . . . The Greeks conceive of *techne*, producing, in terms of letting appear." Heidegger does not note that the primary meaning of *tiktō* is to engender or give birth.

7. *Iliad* 2.214.

8. *Iliad* 24.622.

9. *Odyssey* 8.488–493.

10. There was, of course, grammar as embodied in usage, but grammar as we understand the word—a discipline involving the classification of parts of speech—did not yet exist.

11. The Greeks favored present participles, using them ubiquitously both as adjectives and as nouns (to apply grammatical classifications that did not yet exist when the language was formed), and this is something that underscores the Greek consciousness of emergence. A particularly good example is the word *phainomenon*, which is the medio-passive present participle of the verb *phainō* (come to light). *Phainomena*, literally, are "comings to light," not phenomena or "appearances."

12. In Homer where *soma*, the later term for body, means corpse, *chrōs* (skin) is the word used to designate the living human body: "and *chrōs* does not mean skin in the anatomical sense (the skin or pelt that can be skinned off an animal, *derma*) but skin in the sense of a surface that is the bearer of colour and visibility" (Voegelin 1956–87, 2:102). For a similar assessment, see also Snell 1982, p. 6.

13. Translators have Homeric men *array* themselves in armor, whereas they have Homeric women *adorn* themselves with clothes and jewelry—a distinction not present in the Homeric vocabulary, where the verb **kosmeō** is used for both; a distinction, moreover, that carries unfortunate suggestions about the superfluity of feminine **kosmos**, and of the whole notion of ornament itself. Nevertheless, it is true that **kosmos** refers far more frequently to feminine attire than to masculine attire.

14. *Iliad* 14.170ff.

15. The Loeb translation (A. T. Murray) reads "when she had decked her body with all adornment."

16. Homeric hymn to Artemis 15. The Loeb translation (Hugh G. Evelyn-White) has "and heads and leads the dances gracefully arrayed."

17. **Polys d'hypo kosmos orōren aiglēs lampousēs** (Homeric hymn to Selene 4), which Hugh G. Evelyn-White renders "great is the beauty that ariseth from her shining light."

18. See Kahn 1960, pp. 221ff. Kahn's appendix on **kosmos** (pp. 219–230) is a very helpful survey.

19. Vernant 1982, ch. 8.

20. See Anaximander B1, above: ". . . some different boundless nature, from which all the heavens arise and the **kosmoi** within them."

21. The possibility of understanding Anaximander's book as an architectural treatise will be discussed in the conclusion of this essay.

22. Frontisi-Ducroux 1975, p. 78.

23. For a recent, very thorough study of **daidala** and its applications, see also Morris 1992, part I.

24. The form and matter opposition is one that Heidegger takes great exception to in his essay "The Origin of the Work of Art." Cf. Heidegger 1971, pp. 26ff.

25. *Iliad* 7.418, 11.155; *Odyssey* 5.257, 9.234, 17.316; and Herodotus, 1.203.

26. "And the nymph clothed herself in a long white robe, finely woven [*argypheon*] and beautiful, and about her waist she cast a fair girdle of gold, and on her head a veil above" (*Odyssey* 5.233–235). Here too the **kosmos** of feminine attire reflects or is reflected by the **kosmos** of making.

27. *Odyssey* 5.243–248.

28. See Casson 1963 and 1991.

29. Casson 1963, pp. 28–29.

30. Ibid., p. 32.

31. By the second century A.D., *hylē* had become a medical term referring to the excretions of the human body.

32. As in *Iliad* 7.418 and *Odyssey* 9.234.

33. On sacrificial practices see especially Detienne and Vernant 1989, but also Burkert 1972a, Durand 1986, and Hersey 1988.

34. Linear B, the earliest written form of the Greek language, preserved on clay tablets of the Mycenaean era, dates from 1200 B.C. or earlier.

35. See above, and *Odyssey* 5.361.

36. See especially Lovejoy 1936.

37. On the proportions of Anaximander's cosmology, see Kahn 1960, pp. 86ff., and Kirk, Raven, and Schofield 1983, pp. 134–137.

38. Kirk, Raven, and Schofield, who question the existence of the celestial sphere, base their doubts on the assumption that the model would have been an attempt to illustrate an abstract cosmological theory—that practice is applied theory, in effect. They claim that the theory, being very complex, would have been impossible to illustrate. My speculation that the model came first immediately dispels this objection, since a very complex theory can be developed from a relatively simple model. There need be no one-to-one correspondence.

39. Vitruvius 1.6.2. The translation is my own. An aeolipyle is a pneumatic instrument illustrating the force with which vapor generated by heat in a closed vessel rushes out through a narrow aperture. It was first described by Hero of Alexandria. An *inventio*, in Latin, is a discovery (from *invenio*, I find) as well as an invention in the modern English sense of the term.

40. Ibid.

41. The identity of Homer and the dating of his epics continues to be a highly controversial issue. For an excellent summary see Voegelin 1956–87, 2:68ff. Voegelin's opinion is that the earliest date for the *Iliad* is about 750 B.C., with the *Odyssey* slightly later.

42. Hesiod *Theogony* 575.

43. Frontisi-Ducroux 1975, pp. 52ff.

44. On the adjective **poikilos** see also Carson 1986, p. 24.

45. From **phainō**, come to light.

46. On Pherecydes, see Jaeger 1947, pp. 66ff., Kirk, Raven, and Schofield 1983, pp. 50ff., Vlastos 1952, and Kahn's "Note: The First Greek Prose Treatise" at the conclusion of his book on Anaximander (Kahn 1960).

47. Grenfell and Hunt, *Greek Papyri* ser. II, no. 11, p. 23, cited in Kirk, Raven, and Schofield 1983, p. 61.

48. Cf. Heidegger 1971, p. 159, and above.

49. *Odyssey* 7.94; cf. Morris 1992, p. 228.

50. *Odyssey* 13.311–313.

51. See Frontisi-Ducroux 1975, p. 103.

52. For the Daedalus legend, see Diodorus Siculus 4.76–80, Ovid *Metamorphoses* 8.151–259, and various locations in Pausanias' *Description of Greece*. Recent secondary sources include, especially, Frontisi-Ducroux 1975, part II, pp. 83ff., and Morris 1992. The present very cursory summary does not account for the various versions of the story. As noted earlier, Morris argues that the Athenian phase of Daedalus' career was interpolated by the Athenians themselves during the classical period.

53. Past tense of the verb *askeō* (work curiously, form by art), frequently used in Homer with reference to the making of things that are *daidala*.

54. *Iliad* 18.590–605.

55. See also Morris 1992, p. 14.

56. In *Iliad* 16.183, Hermes is said to have fallen in love with Polymele "when his eyes had sight of her amid the singing maidens, in the *choros* of Artemis," which the Loeb translator (A. T. Murray) renders as the "dancing-floor of Artemis"; but in the context *choros* is more likely to mean "dance," especially since three lines earlier Polymele is described as being "fair in the dance [*choros*]." Moreover, in another location (Homeric hymn to Aphrodite 118), Loeb (Hugh G. Evelyn-White) translates the *choros* of Artemis as the dance of Artemis.

57. *Nausiklutoi*. *Odyssey* 8.369.

58. *Odyssey* 7.127.

59. *Odyssey* 8.248.

60. This Demodocus is the same minstrel who sings so exceedingly **kata kosmon** of the fate of the Achaeans in the passage (*Odyssey* 8.489) cited earlier.

61. *Odyssey* 8.258–264.

62. *Odyssey* 8.340.

63. Diodorus Siculus 4.77.

64. **a-poros**: without passage.

65. Alexander Pope's inaccurate but beautiful translation of the **choros** passage in the *Iliad* describes the movement of Ariadne's dance thus:
> Now all at once they rise, at once descend,
> With well-taught feet: now shape, in oblique ways,
> Confusedly regular, the moving maze.

66. See Rykwert 1988, pp. 143ff.

67. Aeschylus *Eumenides* 631–645; cf. Morris 1992, p. 60.

68. Aeschylus *Agamemnon* 1382; cf. Morris 1992, pp. 60–61 and note 1.

69. On labyrinths in general, see Doob 1990, among others.

70. See above (chapter II, at note 95) on **horaō**, **oida**, and **eidos**.

71. There are some who view the creation myth of Plato's *Timaeus* as the imposition of **kosmos** on **chaos**, but these are not, in fact, Plato's terms. First of all the word **chaos** does not even appear in the dialogue, and secondly, when Timaeus' God brings all that is visible into order out of disorder (30a), the phrase is **eis taxin auto ēgagen ek tēs ataxias**, with **taxis** and its opposite, **ataxis**, the words for order and disorder, respectively.

72. Ovid *Metamorphoses* Book I.

73. "Before the sea was, and the lands, and the sky that hangs over all, the face of Nature showed alike in her whole round, which state men have called chaos [*quem dicere chaos*]: a crude, confused and shapeless mass [*rudis indigesta moles*], nothing at all save lifeless bulk, and warring seeds of ill-matched elements heaped in one" (Ovid *Metamorphoses* 1.5–9). The second-century A.D. Greek sophist Lucian also interpreted **chaos** as disordered shapeless matter (cf. Kirk, Raven, and Schofield 1983, pp. 36–37), but by the second century A.D. Greece had already been part of the Roman Empire for some time. Ovid predates Lucian by over a century.

74. Hesiod *Theogony* 116.

75. Hesiod *Theogony* 700.

76. See Kirk, Raven, and Schofield 1983, p. 38; Vernant 1985, pp. 377ff.

77. Hesiod *Theogony* 736ff. and 831ff.

78. Jaeger (1947, p. 13) calls the opposition between **chaos** and **kosmos** "a purely modern invention." With Ovid in mind, I would call it a Roman one.

79. Pausanias claims an actual marble dancing floor in Knossos to be the one referred to in Homer: "at Knossos, at which place is also Ariadne's Dance mentioned by Homer in the *Iliad*, carved in relief on white marble" (Pausanias 9.40.3–4). Cf. Frontisi-Ducroux 1975, p. 136, and Morris 1992, pp. 248–249.

80. **Prōtistos** is the superlative of the adverb **prōtos**, at the first. Hesiod *Theogony* 116.

81. Diodorus Siculus 4.77.5.

82. Ovid *Metamorphoses* 8.193–195.

83. Ibid. 204–208.

84. Diodorus Siculus 4.77.7. The reference cannot be to Ovid, since Diodorus predates him by a century, but must be to other mythographic sources now lost.

85. Pausanias 9.11.4.

86. Frontisi-Ducroux 1975, pp. 152ff.

87. If Thales, and not Anaximander, is indeed considered the first philosopher, and if Thales did indeed write the "Nautical Star Guide" Simplicius credits him with, then one might conceivably claim that the first philosophical treatise was, in fact, a treatise on navigation.

88. Hesiod *Works and Days* 628–629.

89. Hesiod, fr. 205; in R. Merkelbach and M. L. West, *Fragmenta Hesiodea* (Oxford, 1967), as cited and translated by Morris 1992, p. 193.

90. *Odyssey* 11.125. See also Euripides' *Helen* 146–149 and 666–668, where oars are referred to as wings; cf. Hart 1988, p. 92.

91. Cf. Hart 1988, p. 89. Hart has also pointed out that wings were imagined to move like the oars of a ship. On wings and navigation see his chapter 3: "Horizontal Flight."

92. *Odyssey* 7.36.

93. *Iliad* 16.773.

94. See also *Iliad* 5.171 and 20.68.

95. *Iliad* 19.386.

96. On **mētis**, see especially Detienne and Vernant 1978.

97. *Odyssey* 12.234ff.

98. Christopher Marlowe, *Tamburlaine the Great*, 2.7.18–20.

99. Robert Browning, "Andrea del Sarto," 97–98.

100. Ovid was widely read in the Renaissance and greatly influenced many English Renaissance poets, including Marlowe, who refers explicitly to the Icarus legend in the opening lines of *Dr. Faustus.*

101. From the verb *histēmi*, I set up.

102. Homeric hymn to Hephaestus.

103. For a discussion of the difference between *ergasthai* (to work) and *ponein* (to labor), see Arendt 1958, chapter 3.

104. See Glotz 1929, pp. 33ff.

105. *Odyssey* 17.381ff.

106. This refers to the benches on which the oarsmen sat.

107. *Odyssey* 9.125ff.

108. This is something that Giambattista Vico (1670–1744), whose *New Science* is, among other things, a seminal exploration of the relationship between artifact and institution, understood particularly well.

109. Pausanias 3.11.9.

110. Herodotus 6.27.

111. *Odyssey* 8.258ff.

112. See Glotz 1929, p. 91.

113. On Hippodamus, see Aristotle *Politics* 1267b24ff., Vernant 1985, pp. 202ff., Rykwert 1988, pp. 85ff., and Burns 1976.

114. Aristotle *Politics* 1267b24.

115. Ibid. 1267b30.

116. Dinsmoor 1941, p. 126. Cf. Burford 1972, p. 167.

117. Xenophon *Memorabilia* 3.10.1–15. Cf. Burford 1972, p. 156.

118. Diodorus Siculus 4.78.2.

119. Diodorus Siculus 4.30.1; cf. Morris 1992, p. 207. The translation here is Morris's.

IV

Between Movement and Fixity: The Place for Order

1. "The need implied in colonization to create a society *ex novo* required conceptualizing what the social unit was and what the ideal type should be" (Malkin 1987, p. 263).

2. Ibid.

3. A similar classification was made by Vallet and appears to have become standard.

4. Physically, the **polis** consisted of the **asty**, town, and its **chōra**, territory.

5. *Iliad* 23.521.

6. *Iliad* 17.394.

7. *Iliad* 16.68.

8. *Iliad* 4.505, 12.406, 13.324, 16.588, 16.629, 17.101, 17.316.

9. The transliteration convention adopted here uses *ō* for omega and *o*, without the macron, for omicron. **Chōros** and **choros** are two different words in Greek, although there is a level where their senses appear to converge.

10. *Iliad* 3.315.

11. *Iliad* 3.344.

12. For example, *Odyssey* 21.142: "Rise up in order all you of our company, from left to right, beginning from the place [*chōros*] where the cupbearer pours the wine."

13. Aristotle *Physics* 212a27.

14. See, especially, Harold Cherniss' discussion in *Aristotle's Criticism of Presocratic Philosophy* (1935).

15. Aristotle *Physics* 209b14ff.

16. Plato *Timaeus* 52a.

17. Ibid. 52b.

18. Roth 1916, p. 284.

19. Garland 1987, p. 13. In fact, the site where Themistocles built the Piraeus lacked just about everything Vitruvius (Book I, chapter 4) says should be sought to ensure the *salubritas* of the site for a city.

20. The cult of the Thracian goddess Bendis, whose festival, the Bendeia, Socrates goes down to the Piraeus to see at the opening of the *Republic*, is the best known of these. Eric Voegelin claims (1956–87, 3:59–60) that the Piraeus in the *Republic* is a reflection both of Hades and of the cave with its shadow play: "The empty freedom of the Piraeus, with its celebration of the chthonian divinity, becomes the empty freedom of Arete in Hades, and they both blend into the play of shadows in the cave."

21. Thucydides 2.36.2. Cf. Garland 1987, p. 15.

22. There are at least three parallels for this kind of umbilical attachment. Around 560 B.C., the Ephesians, while under siege by the Lydian king Croesus, "dedicated their city to Artemis; this they did by attaching rope to the city wall from the temple of the goddess,

standing seven furlongs away from the ancient city which was then being besieged" (Herodotus 1.26). A little later, Polycrates, tyrant of Samos, added Rhenia, an island very close to Delos, "to his other island conquests during his period of naval ascendancy, [and] dedicated it to the Delian Apollo and bound it with a chain to Delos" (Thucydides 3.104.2). Also the fountain of Arethusa, near Syracuse, an eighth-century Corinthian foundation in Sicily, was believed to be a resurgence of the river Alpheus (Pindar *Pythian* 2.5 and 12; Pausanias 5.14.6) and was, as François de Polignac points out (1984, p. 104), a manifestation for the colonists of an umbilical link "between the land and the gods of Greece and the new horizon of hellenism." Long walls connecting the city to its port also existed at Corinth and at Megara, although these were nowhere near as long as the Athenian ones. See Adam 1982.

23. Plutarch *Themistocles* 19.4. The reference to Aristophanes is to *Knights* 815.

24. Aristotle *Politics* 1331a28–30, as translated by Ernest Barker in his *The Politics of Aristotle* (Oxford, 1958), pp. 309–310. Cf. Malkin 1987, pp. 147–148. Aristotle, who wrote the passage nearly three hundred years after the colonization period, was talking about the **polis** in general and not about colonial cities as such.

25. Aristotle *Politics* 1331a28–30: *eiē d'an toioutos ho topos hostis epiphanian te exei pros tēn tēs aretēs thesin ikanōs kai pros ta geitniōnta merē tēs poleōs erymnoterōs.*

26. Callimachus, hymn to Apollo 55–57; cf. Malkin 1987, p. 142.

27. *Glaukōpis*, bright-eyed or of the flashing eyes, is a fixed epithet for Athena.

28. Even the Ionian cities were, in a sense, colonies, since they were established by Achaeans who fled continental Greece after the Dorian invasion. See also Malkin 1987, p. 114: "Greeks in the fifth century did not distinguish between what we may define as the migratory period of the Dark Ages and the colonization. The former was conceived in terms of the latter."

29. Thucydides 2.36.2.

30. Herodotus 7.161; cf. Morris 1992, p. 329. The claim, says Morris, is allied to a racial one: "The Athenians have never been invaded, hence their blood has never been contaminated by barbarians (see Plato, *Menexenus* 245d). This resistance to outside invasion argues from nature what happened in history: because the Athenians defended their territory, and 'saved' Greece from the Persians, it became logical to imagine an infinite past when this was true."

31. Thucydides 1.93.5.

32. See de Polignac 1984, pp. 88–89.

33. That the **polis** did not emerge in Athens but was, like almost everything else in the fifth-century city, an import, made for special difficulties. See Voegelin 1956–87, 2:268ff. For a recent discussion of Periclean Athens see Robert Jan van Pelt, "Athenian Assurance," in van Pelt and Westfall 1991, pp. 168–261.

34. See Kerényi 1978, p. 29: "An acceptable meaning for the word 'Athene' is yielded only if one dares to reach for an old forgotten vocabulary, which in several instances has turned out to be the common property of the pre-Greek inhabitants of Greece and the Etruscans of Italy. From the sacred language of the Etruscans have been preserved such words as *althanulus*, 'holy vessel of the priest'; *atena*, 'clay beaker for use in sacrifice'; *attana*, 'pan'." Kerényi connects this etymology to the "extraordinary significance of ceramics for prehistoric and historical Athens."

35. The inventory is that given by Herington 1955, p. 23.

36. Pausanias 1.24.5.

37. Pausanias 1.26.6.

38. See Kerényi 1978, pp. 40ff.

39. See Farnell 1896, pp. 297ff.

40. Pausanias 1.29.1: "Near the Hill of Ares is shown a ship built for the procession of the Panathenaea. This ship, I suppose, has been surpassed in size by others, but I know of no builder who has beaten the vessel at Delos, with its nine banks of oars below deck."

41. Homeric hymn to Selene 4. See above, chapter III, at note 17.

42. *Iliad* 6.294–295.

43. *Iliad* 6.309–311.

44. *Iliad* 7.436–444.

45. See also Mossé 1980.

46. *Odyssey* 8.369.

47. Demetrius Phalereus was a rhetorician of the fourth century B.C.

48. Plutarch *Theseus* 23.1.

49. Plato *Phaedo* 58b: "This is the ship, as the Athenians say, in which Theseus once went to Crete with the fourteen youths and maidens, and saved them and himself. Now the Athenians made a vow to Apollo, as the story goes, that if they were saved they would send a mission every year to Delos."

50. See Farnell 1896, p. 295, and Hammond 1986, p. 165.

51. Plutarch *Cimon* 8 and *Theseus* 35, 36; Pausanias 3.3.7. Cf. Malkin 1987, p. 201.

52. See also Morris 1992, pp. 336ff., "'This Other Herakles': The Invention of Theseus."

53. Leon Battista Alberti, *On the Art of Building in Ten Books*, 7.1 (Alberti 1988, 189).

54. Plutarch *Themistocles* 11.4.

55. Themistocles, Cimon, and Pericles.

56. I.e., the long walls that linked Athens to the Piraeus.

57. Plato *Gorgias* 519a. Cf. Garland 1987, p. 69. The translation here is Garland's.

58. Some of them, such as Critias and Charmides, were his former pupils.

59. Plutarch *Themistocles* 19.4.

60. Garland 1987, p. 69. On Plato's (and Socrates') antipathy to democracy and sea power, cf. also Kahn 1963, especially p. 224.

61. Plato *Laws* 654b.

62. Ibid. Convictions about the political relevance of music survive well into the Renaissance:

> The man that hath no music in himself
> Nor is not mov'd with concord of sweet sounds,
> Is fit for treasons, stratagems, and spoils: . . .
> (Shakespeare, The Merchant of Venice, 5.1.83–85)

63. In Homeric Greece, the ***megaron*** was a large hall, the chief room of the palace, which contained the sacred hearth. ***Megara*** did not become freestanding until the eighth century.

64. Cf. Pliny the Elder *Natural History* 36.31: "The Greek word for the surrounding colonnade is 'pteron,' 'wing.'" For documentation on the early Greek temples see Burkert 1985, pp. 88ff., Coldstream 1977, pp. 321ff., Coulton 1977, pp. 30ff., Dinsmoor 1950, pp. 62ff., Hurwit 1985, pp. 74ff., Lawrence 1983, pp. 115ff., Martin 1988, pp. 39ff., and Scully 1979. On the Heraion at Samos, see especially Walter 1976.

65. Long thought to be the first peripteral temple, the Samian Heraion's claim has been superseded by that of a very early (tenth-century) recently excavated temple at Lefkandi, as well as by a later one at

Eretria. Both Lefkandi and Eretria are in Euboea and the Euboean cities of Chalkis and Eretria were among the first colonizers. It is my suspicion that, with further research, the temple at Lefkandi may well prove to have become winged for reasons similar to those I shall argue for the case of the temple of Hera at Samos. A late ninth- or early eighth-century temple has also been discovered at Thermon. See also Hurwit 1985, p. 77 note 7, on this matter.

66. Coldstream 1977, p. 327. Coldstream echoes the opinion voiced by Dinsmoor (1950, p. 62).

67. Hurwit 1985, pp. 76–77.

68. Coulton 1977, p. 31.

69. Scully 1979, p. 50.

70. Personified, *hestia*, the hearth, is Hestia the goddess of the hearth. See especially Jean-Pierre Vernant's discussion of Hermes and Hestia in Vernant 1985, pp. 155ff.

71. See especially chapter three, "The Sacred Fire and the Public Hearth," in Malkin 1987.

72. This kind of troping was, if Hersey's argument is accepted, a pervasive feature of the development of temple architecture. The identification of *naus* and *naos* has had a long history in Western architecture, and indeed the central bay of a church continues to be called its nave, from the Latin *navis*, ship. In French the entire church is often referred to as *le vaisseau*, the vessel.

73. *Odyssey* 11.120.

74. On the extraordinarily sophisticated level of Samian craftsmanship see, among others, Richter 1949, pp. 102ff., and Burford 1972, pp. 191ff.

75. Vitruvius 7.Pref.12.

76. See Casson 1991, pp. 77–78.

77. Ibid.

78. Pliny the Elder *Natural History* 34.83.

79. See Frontisi-Ducroux 1975, pp. 132–134.

80. Plato *Ion* 533a; cf. Morris 1992, p. 236.

81. Pausanias 10.5.9–10. Pausanias also mentions a third temple made of bronze.

82. Frontisi-Ducroux 1975, pp. 167–168.

83. I am grateful to George Hersey for pointing this out to me.

84. Liddell and Scott, s.v. **aetos**.

85. See Casson 1991, p. 79.

86. The Victory of Samothrace illustrated here is the best known, but there were others. See for example Casson 1991, figure 33.

87. Vitruvius 1.2.1: *constat*: stands with, corresponds to.

88. Vitruvius 1.2.3–4.

89. Vitruvius 6.2.2.

90. Pollitt 1972, p. 57.

91. "Shapely" is another fairly common, although less accurate. translation of **euērēs**.

92. It takes Penelope three years to weave the funeral cloth that keeps the suitors waiting (*Odyssey* 2.106). This, according to Elizabeth Barber's calculation (1991, p. 363), is about the time it would have taken an ancient Greek woman working alone to weave a cloth with the dimension and complexity of Penelope's.

93. Aorist passive infinitive of *histēmi*, I set up. According to Hesiod, on the twelfth day of the month a woman "should set up [*stēsaito*] her loom and get forward with her work." Penelope in the second book of the *Odyssey* "set up in her halls a great loom [*stēsamenē megan histon*]" in order to begin weaving the cloth that saves her household (*Odyssey* 2.94).

94. See Barber 1991, pp. 91ff.

95. For example, rows of loom weights found between two post holes in a floor at Troy, level IIg, are taken to be firm evidence of the existence of at least one Aegean bronze age warp-weighted loom, which apparently was consumed by fire, along with the fabric in the process of being woven on it. See Barber 1991, p. 93.

96. Judith Brown, "A Note on the Division of Labor by Sex," *American Anthropologist* 72, 1 (1970): 1075. Cited in Barber 1991, p. 289.

97. See Malkin 1987, chapter 3.

98. *Histia*, as noted earlier, is the Ionian spelling for *hestia*.

99. It has often been remarked that to be a citizen of fifth-century Athens was no sinecure. Citizens spent most of their time governing themselves. Self-government, like hand weaving, was very time-consuming.

100. By Coulton (1977, p. 49) and Dinsmoor (1950, p. 67), among others.

101. See Barber 1991, pp. 83ff.

102. See Cole 1967, and Burford 1972, pp. 186ff.

103. Vitruvius 2.1.3.

104. See, especially, Pollitt 1972, pp. 75ff., but also Dinsmoor 1950, chapter 5, and Coulton 1977, pp. 108ff., among others. The first detailed study, F. C. Penrose's *An Investigation of the Principles of Athenian Architecture*, was published in 1851 (2d ed. London, 1888).

105. Vitruvius is not speaking explicitly of the Parthenon, but he does cite Ictinus, its architect, as one of his sources in the preface to Book VII.

106. Vitruvius 6.2.4.

107. Euclid's *Optics* was written around 300 B.C.

108. Vitruvius 6.2.5.

109. Scully 1979, p. 184.

110. Hesiod *Works and Days* 628.

111. Pausanias 1.24.7.

112. Pausanias 3.15.7: "Opposite this temple [of Hipposthenes] is an old image of Enyalius in fetters. The idea the Lacedaemonians express by this image is the same as the Athenians express by their Wingless Victory." Cf. Frontisi-Ducroux 1975, p. 104.

113. See especially A. Mavrikios, "Aesthetic Analysis Concerning the Curvature of the Parthenon," in Bruno 1974, pp. 199ff.

114. Vernant 1982, p. 122. **Isonomia**, literally, is equal law (**nomos**), or equality before the law.

115. Herodotus 3.142. Cf. Vernant 1982, p. 127. The translation here is Vernant's.

116. As far as I know, I am the only one to have done so. Perhaps Vitruvius' Greek sources talked about these connections, but if they did Vitruvius must have missed the point, for although he talks about clocks and machines at length, he has very little to say about naval architecture or about looms. The Romans were much less of a seafaring nation than the Greeks.

117. Thucydides 7.77.7. Cf. Rykwert 1988, p. 23, and Hurwit 1985, p. 73. Similar sentiments are expressed, among others, by Alcaeus (fr. 22); Sophocles (*Oedipus Tyrannus* 56); Aeschylus (*Persians* 349), and Plutarch (*Lycurgus* 19); cf. note 1 in vol. 4, p. 158, of the Loeb Thucydides.

—————————————— V ——————————————

Conclusion

1. Aristotle *Metaphysics* 981a30–b2.

2. Vitruvius 1.1.15–16.

3. Vitruvius 7.Pref.12. This is the third, dipteral, Samian Heraion spoken of earlier. See also Coulton 1977, p. 24.

4. Vitruvius 1.1.4. This translation is my own.

5. Aristotle *Metaphysics* 982b12.

6. See, for example, *Iliad* 15.410ff.: "But as the carpenter's line [**stathmē**] makes straight a ship's timber in the hands of a cunning workman, well skilled [**eu sophiēs**] in all manner of craft by the **eidos** [image, certain knowledge] of Athena . . ."

7. *Iliad* 18.599.

8. Xenophon *Memorabilia* 4.2.33: "Have you not heard how Daedalus was seized by Minos because of his wisdom [**dia tēn sophian**], and was forced to be his slave, and was robbed of his country and his liberty, and essaying to escape with his son, lost the boy and could not save himself, but was carried off to the barbarians and again lived as a slave there?" Socrates' point is that **sophia** can have unpleasant consequences, as indeed it did for himself.

9. Plutarch *Themistocles* 2.4. Mnesiphilus, who dates from the end of the sixth century, was a forerunner of the sophists Plato so despised.

10. That **sophia** and **technē** were complementary is made very clear in the Homeric hymn to Hermes. Hermes gives Apollo the lyre, which he has invented, and says,

    *Sing well with this clear-voiced companion in your hands; for you are skilled [**epistamenos**] in good well-ordered utterance [**kala kai eu kata kosmon agoreuein**]. From now on bring it confidently to the rich feast and lovely dance. . . . Whoso with **technē** and **sophia** enquires of it cunningly, him it teaches through its sound all manner of things that delight the mind. (478ff.).*
    A few lines later (511), Hermes "found out another **technē** of **sophia** and made himself pipes whose sound is heard afar."

11. Harrison 1912, p. 500.

12. See Pausanias 1.24.5: "All the figures in the gable over the entrance to the temple called the Parthenon relate to the birth of Athena."

13. Aeschylus *Eumenides* 562ff., cited in Harrison 1912, p. 501:
    This too I tell you, mark how plain my speech
    The mother is no parent of her child
    Only the nurse of the young seed within her.
    The male is the parent, she as outside friend
    Cherishes the plant, if fate allows its bloom.
    Proof will I bring of this my argument.
    A Father needs no mother's help. She [i.e., Athena] stands
    Child of Olympian Zeus, to be my witness,
    Reared never in the darkness of the womb,
    Yet fairer plant than any heaven begot.

14. It is to my mind no accident that Pythagoras, the source of so much of Western thinking about **harmonia** and **kosmos**, came from Samos, known in the archaic period for the high level of its craftsmanship. He was, like Socrates, the son of a craftsman: his father was a gem carver. Although we do not know the profession of Anaximander's father, his name, curiously enough, was Praxiades (Diogenes Laertius 2.1.; cf. Kirk, Raven, and Schofield 1983, p. 101).

15. Leon Battista Alberti, *On the Art of Building in Ten Books*, 7.3 (Alberti 1988, p. 195).

16. Plato *Gorgias* 507e.

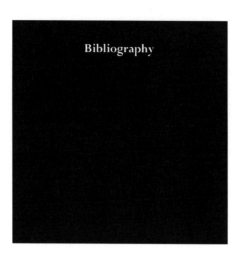

Bibliography

Editions of Classical Authors

Aeschylus *Agamemnon, Eumenides*. In *Aeschylus with an English Translation by Herbert Weir Smyth*. Loeb Classical Library. 2 vols. Cambridge, Mass., 1963.

Aëtius. In Diels 1952. Cited and translated in Kirk, Raven, and Schofield 1983.

Agathemerus. In Diels 1952. Cited and translated in Kirk, Raven, and Schofield 1983.

Aristotle *Metaphysics*. In *The Metaphysics with an English Translation by Hugh Tredennick*. Loeb Classical Library. 2 vols. London, 1933–35.

Aristotle *On the Heavens*. In *On the Heavens with an English Translation by W. K. C. Guthrie*. Loeb Classical Library. Cambridge, Mass., 1939.

Aristotle *Physics*. In *The Physics with an English Translation by Philip H. Wicksteed and Francis M. Cornford*. Loeb Classical Library. 2 vols. London, 1929–34.

Aristotle *Politics*. In *The Politics with an English Translation by H. Rackham*. Loeb Classical Library. Cambridge, Mass., 1959.

Callimachus. In *Callimachus, Hymns and Epigrams and Lycophron Translated into English by A. W. Muir*. Loeb Classical Library. Revised edition. Cambridge, Mass., 1955.

Diodorus Siculus. In *Diodorus of Sicily with an English Translation by C. H. Oldfather*. Loeb Classical Library. 12 vols. London and New York, 1933–67.

Diogenes Laertius. In *Lives of the Eminent Philosophers with an English Translation by R. D. Hicks*. Loeb Classical Library. 2 vols. London and New York, 1925.

Heraclitus. In Diels 1952. Cited and translated in Kirk, Raven, and Schofield 1983.

Herodotus. In *Herodotus with an English Translation by A. D. Godley*. Loeb Classical Library. 4 vols. Cambridge, Mass., and London, 1926–38.

Hesiod *Theogony*, *Works and Days*. In *Hesiod, the Homeric Hymns and Homerica with an English Translation by H. G. Evelyn-White*. Loeb Classical Library. Cambridge, Mass., and London, 1914.

Homeric hymns. In *Hesiod, the Homeric Hymns and Homerica with an English Translation by H. G. Evelyn-White*. Loeb Classical Library. Cambridge, Mass., and London, 1914.

Homer *Iliad*. In *The Iliad with an English Translation by A. T. Murray*. Loeb Classical Library. 2 vols. Cambridge, Mass., and London, 1924.

Homer *Odyssey*. In *The Odyssey with an English Translation by A. T. Murray*. Loeb Classical Library. 2 vols. Cambridge, Mass., and London, 1919.

Hyppolytus. In Diels 1952. Cited and translated by Kirk, Raven, and Schofield 1983.

Ovid *Metamorphoses*. In *The Metamorphoses with an English Translation by Frank Justus Miller*. Loeb Classical Library. London, 1921.

Pausanias. In *Pausanias, Description of Greece with an English Translation by W. H. S. Jones*. Loeb Classical Library. 4 vols. London and New York, 1918–35.

Plato *Alcibiades*, *Euthyphro*, *Meno*. In *The Dialogues of Plato*. Trans. B. Jowett. 2 vols. New York, 1937.

Plato *Gorgias*, *Hippias Major*, *Ion*, *Laws*, *Phaedo*, *Timaeus*. In *Plato with an English Translation by H. N. Fowler and an Introduction by W. R. M. Lamb*. Loeb Classical Library. 10 vols. London and New York, 1914–29.

Pliny the Elder *Natural History*. In *Natural History with an English Translation by H. Rackham, W. H. S. Jones and D. E. Eichholz*. Loeb Classical Library. 10 vols. Cambridge, Mass., and London, 1938–63.

Plutarch *Cimon*, *Themistocles*. In *Plutarch, Lives with an English Translation by B. Perrin*. Loeb Classical Library. 11 vols. London, 1914–26.

Plutarch *Theseus*. In *Plutarch's Lives*. Trans. John Dryden, rev. Arthur Hugh Clough. Modern Library. New York, n.d.

Shield of Heracles. In *Hesiod, the Homeric Hymns and Homerica with an English Translation by H. G. Evelyn-White*. Loeb Classical Library. Cambridge, Mass., and London, 1914.

Suda. In Diels 1952. Cited and translated in Kirk, Raven, and Schofield 1983.

Theognis. In *Théognis: Poèmes élégiaques*. Ed. and trans. into French by Jean Carrière. 2d ed. Paris, 1962.

Thucydides. In *History of the Peloponnesian War with an English Translation by Charles Forster Smith*. Loeb Classical Library. 4 vols. London and New York, 1919–23.

Vitruvius. In *Vitruvius, on Architecture*. Ed. and trans. Frank Granger. Loeb Classical Library. 2 vols. Cambridge, Mass., and London, 1931.

Xenophon *Memorabilia*. In *Memorabilia and Oeconomicus with an English Translation by O. J. Todd*. Loeb Classical Library. 7 vols. Cambridge, Mass., and London, 1979.

─────────── Modern Works ───────────

Adam, Jean-Pierre. 1982. *L'architecture militaire grecque*. Paris.

Alberti, Leon Battista. 1988. *On the Art of Building in Ten Books*. Trans. Joseph Rykwert, Neil Leach, and Robert Tavernor. Cambridge, Mass.

Arendt, Hannah. 1958. *The Human Condition*. Chicago.

Ashmole, Bernard. 1972. *Architect and Sculptor in Classical Greece*. London.

Barber, E. J. W. 1991. *Prehistoric Textiles*. Princeton.

Barnes, J. 1979. *The Presocratic Philosophers*. 2 vols. London.

Bervé, H., H. Gruben, and M. Hirmer. N.d. *Greek Temples, Theatres and Shrines*. New York.

Bill, Clarence P. 1901. "Notes on the Greek *Theōros* and *Theōria*." *Transactions and Proceedings of the American Philological Association* 32:196–204.

Bollack, Jean. 1968. "Une histoire de **sophiē**." *Revue des études grecques* 81:550–554.

Bruno, Vincent J. 1974. *The Parthenon*. New York.

Bunbury, E. H. 1959. *A History of Ancient Geography*. 2d ed. 2 vols. New York.

Burford, A. 1972. *Craftsmen in Greek and Roman Society*. London.

Burkert, Walter. 1972a. *Homo Necans: The Anthropology of Ancient Greek Sacrificial Ritual and Myth*. Trans. from the German by Peter Bing. Berkeley.

Burkert, Walter. 1972b. *Lore and Science in Ancient Pythagoreanism*. Trans. Edwin L. Minor, Jr. Cambridge, Mass.

Burkert, Walter. 1985. *Greek Religion*. Trans. from the German by John Raffan. Cambridge, Mass.

Burnet, John. 1930. *Early Greek Philosophy*. 4th ed. London.

Burns, A. 1976. "Hippodamus and the Planned City." *Historia* 25:414–428.

Carson, Anne. 1986. *Eros the Bittersweet*. Princeton.

Casson, Lionel. 1963. "Ancient Shipbuilding: New Light on an Old Source." *Transactions of the American Philological Association* 194:28–33.

Casson, Lionel. 1991. *The Ancient Mariners: Seafarers and Sea Fighters of the Mediterranean in Ancient Times*. 2d ed. Princeton.

Cherniss, Harold. 1935. *Aristotle's Criticism of Presocratic Philosophy*. Baltimore.

Cleve, Felix M. 1969. *The Giants of Pre-Sophistic Greek Philosophy*. 2 vols. The Hague.

Coldstream, J. N. 1977. *Geometric Greece*. London.

Cole, T. 1967. "Democritus and the Sources of Greek Anthropology." *Philological Monographs* 25. American Philological Association.

Cornford, F. M. 1957. *From Religion to Philosophy*. New York. First published 1912.

Coulton, J. J. 1977. *Ancient Greek Architects at Work*. Ithaca.

Detienne, Marcel, and Jean-Pierre Vernant. 1978. *Cunning Intelligence in Greek Culture and Society*. Trans. from the French by Janet Lloyd. Atlantic Highlands, N.J.

Detienne, Marcel, and Jean-Pierre Vernant. 1989. *The Cuisine of Sacrifice among the Greeks*. With essays by Jean-Louis Durand, Stella Georgoudi, François Hartog and Jesper Svenbro. Trans. from the French by Paula Wissing. Chicago.

Diels, H. 1879. *Doxographi Graeci.* Berlin.

Diels, H. 1952. *Die Fragmente der Vorsokratiker*. 6th ed., with additions and index by W. Kranz. Berlin.

Dinsmoor, William Bell. 1941. "Observations on the Hephaisteion." *Hesperia*, suppl. 5:125ff.

Dinsmoor, William Bell. 1950. *The Architecture of Ancient Greece*. 3d ed. London.

Dodds, E. R. 1951. *The Greeks and the Irrational*. Berkeley.

Donohue, A. A. 1988. *Xoana and the Origins of Greek Sculpture*. Atlanta.

Doob, Penelope Reed. 1990. *The Idea of the Labyrinth*. Ithaca.

Dunbar, Henry. 1962. *A Complete Concordance to the Odyssey of Homer*. New edition, revised and enlarged by Benedetto Marzullo. Hildesheim, Germany.

Durand, Jean-Louis. 1986. *Sacrifice et labour en Grèce ancienne*. Paris and Rome.

Farnell, L. R. 1896. *The Cults of the Greek States*. Oxford.

Frankfort, H. 1951. *Before Philosophy*. Harmondsworth, England.

Freeman, Kathleen. 1946. *The Pre-Socratic Philosophers: A Companion to Diels, Fragmente der Vorsokratiker*. Oxford.

Frontisi-Ducroux, Françoise. 1975. *Dédale: mythologie de l'artisan en Grèce ancienne*. Paris.

Furley, D. J., and R. E. Allen, eds. 1970–75. *Studies in Presocratic Philosophy*. 2 vols. London.

Fustel de Coulanges, Numa Denis. 1955. *The Ancient City*. New York.

Garland, Robert. 1987. *The Piraeus from the Fifth to the First Century B.C.* London.

Gernet, Louis. 1968. *Anthropologie de la Grèce antique*. Paris.

Glotz, Gustave. 1929. *The Greek City and Its Institutions*. Trans. from the French by N. Mallinson. London.

Gottschalk, H. B. 1965. "Anaximander's Apeiron." *Phronesis* 10:37–53.

Graves, Robert. 1960. *The Greek Myths*. 2 vols. Rev. ed. Harmondsworth, England.

Hammond, N. G. L. 1986. *A History of Greece to 322 B.C.* 3d ed. Oxford.

Harrison, J. E. 1912. *Themis: A Study of the Social Origins of Greek Religion*. 2d ed. London.

Harrison, J. E. 1922. *Prolegomena to the Study of Greek Religion*. 3d ed. Cambridge, England.

Hart, Clive. 1988. *Images of Flight*. Berkeley.

Heidegger, Martin. 1950. *An Introduction to Metaphysics*. New Haven.

Heidegger, Martin. 1971. *Poetry, Language, Thought*. New York.

Heidegger, Martin. 1984. *Early Greek Thinking: The Dawn of Western Philosophy*. New York.

Heidel, W. A. 1921. "Anaximander's Book, the Earliest Known Geographical Treatise." *Proceedings of the American Academy of Arts and Sciences* 56, no. 7 (April):239–288.

Heidel, W. A. 1937. *The Frame of the Ancient Greek Maps*. New York.

Herington, C. J. 1955. *Athena Parthenos and Athena Polias*. Manchester.

Hersey, George. 1988. *The Lost Meaning of Classical Architecture*. Cambridge, Mass.

Holloway, R. R. 1960. "Architect and Engineer in Archaic Greece." *Harvard Studies in Classical Philology* 73:281–290.

Hölscher, U. 1970. "Anaximander and the Beginnings of Greek Philosophy." In Furley and Allen 1970–75, 1:281–322. (English translation of an article in *Anfängliches Fragen*, first published in *Hermes* 81 (1953):255–277, 358–417.)

Hurwit, Jeffrey M. 1985. *The Art and Culture of Early Greece 1100–480 B.C.* Ithaca and London.

Jaeger, Werner. 1947. *The Theology of the Early Greek Philosophers*. Trans. from the German for the Gifford Lectures of 1936 by Edward S. Robinson. Oxford.

Johannes, H. 1937. "Die Säulenbasen von Heratempel des Rhoikos." *Mitteilungen des Deutschen Archäologischen Instituts* 62:15–17.

Kahn, Charles H. 1960. *Anaximander and the Origins of Greek Cosmology*. New York.

Kahn, Charles H. 1963. "Plato's Funeral Oration: The Motive of the *Menexenus*." *Classical Philology* 58:220–234.

Kerényi, Karl. 1978. *Athene: Virgin and Mother in Greek Religion*. Trans. from the German by Murray Stein. Zurich.

Kirk, G. S. 1974. *The Nature of the Greek Myths*. Harmondsworth, England.

Kirk, G. S., J. E. Raven, and M. Schofield. 1983. *The Presocratic Philosophers*. 2d ed. Cambridge, England.

Kroll, John H. 1982. "The Ancient Image of Athena Polias." *Hesperia* supplement 20:65–77.

Lawrence, A. W. 1983. *Greek Architecture*. 4th ed. Harmondsworth, England.

Liddell, Henry George, and Robert Scott. 1968. *A Greek-English Lexicon* . . . Rpt. of 9th ed., with a new supplement ed. E. A. Barber et al. Oxford.

Lloyd-Jones, Hugh. 1971. *The Justice of Zeus*. Berkeley.

Lobkowicz, Nicholas. 1967. *Theory and Practice*. Notre Dame, Indiana.

Lovejoy, A. O. 1936. *The Great Chain of Being*. Cambridge, Mass.

Malkin, Irad. 1987. *Religion and Colonization in Ancient Greece*. Leiden.

Martin, R. 1974. *Urbanisme dans la Grèce antique*. Paris.

Martin, R. 1988. *Greek Architecture*. New York.

Morris, Sarah P. 1992. *Daidalos and the Origins of Greek Art*. Princeton.

Mossé, Claude. 1980. "Ithaque ou la naissance de la cité." *Studi di Archeologia e Storia Antica* 2:7–19.

Mugler, C. 1958. "Sur l'histoire de quelques définitions de la géométrie grecque: la surface." *L'antiquité classique,* pp. 76–91.

Murray, Oswyn, and Simon Price, eds. 1990. *The Greek City from Homer to Alexander.* Oxford.

Onians, Richard Broxton. 1951. *The Origins of European Thought about the Body, the Mind, the Soul, the World, Time and Fate.* Cambridge, England.

Pérez-Gómez, Alberto. 1985. "The Myth of Daedalus." *AA Files* 10 (Autumn):49–52.

de Polignac, François. 1984. *La naissance de la cité grecque.* Paris.

Pollitt, J. J. 1972. *Art and Experience in Classical Greece.* Cambridge, England.

Prendergast, G. L. 1962. *A Complete Concordance to the Iliad of Homer.* New edition, revised and enlarged by Benedetto Marzullo. Hildesheim, Germany.

Rausch, Hannelore. 1982. *Theōria.* Munich.

Richter, G. M. A. 1949. *Archaic Greek Art.* New York.

Roth, H. Ling. 1916. "Studies in Primitive Looms." *Journal of the Royal Anthropological Institute* 46:284–309.

Rouse, William Henry Denham. 1902. *Greek Votive Offerings: An Essay in the History of Greek Religion.* Cambridge, England.

Rykwert, Joseph. 1988. *The Idea of a Town.* 2d ed. Cambridge, Mass.

Schachermeyr, F. 1953. "The Genesis of the Greek Polis." *Diogenes,* no. 4:17–30.

Scully, Vincent. 1979. *The Earth, the Temple, and the Gods.* Rev. ed. New Haven.

Seligman, Paul. 1962. *The Apeiron of Anaximander.* New York.

Snell, Bruno. 1982. *The Discovery of the Mind in Greek Philosophy and Literature.* New York.

Snodgrass, A. 1967. *Arms and Armour of the Greeks.* London.

Snodgrass, A. 1977. *Archaeology and the Rise of the Greek City State.* Cambridge, England.

Snodgrass, A. 1981. *Archaic Greece, The Age of Experiment.* Cambridge, England.

Steiner, George. 1978. *Heidegger.* London.

Stone, I. F. 1988. *The Trial of Socrates.* Boston and Toronto.

Thomson, G. 1953. "From Religion to Philosophy." *Journal of Hellenic Studies,* 73:77–84.

Thomson, J. O. 1965. *History of Ancient Geography.* New York.

Vallet, G. 1968. "La cité et son territoire dans les colonies grecques d'occident." *Atti del 7e Convegno di Studi sulla Magna Grecia,* pp. 67–142. Naples.

van Pelt, Robert Jan, and Carroll William Westfall. 1991. *Architectural Principles in the Age of Historicism.* New Haven.

Vermeule, Emily. 1964. *Greece in the Bronze Age.* Chicago.

Vernant, Jean-Pierre. 1974. *Mythe et société en Grèce ancienne.* Paris.

Vernant, Jean-Pierre. 1982. *The Origins of Greek Thought.* Ithaca.

Vernant, Jean-Pierre. 1985. *Mythe et pensée chez les Grecs.* Paris.

Vico, Giambattista. 1968. *The New Science of Giambattista Vico.* Unabridged translation of the third edition (1744), trans. Thomas Goddard Bergin and Max Harold Fisch. Ithaca and London.

Vlastos, G. 1947. "Equality and Justice in Early Greek Cosmologies." *Classical Philology* 42:156–178. (Reprinted in Furley and Allen 1970–75.)

Vlastos, G. 1952. "Theology and Philosophy in Early Greek Thought." *Philosophical Quarterly* 2:97–123. (Reprinted in Furley and Allen 1970–75.)

Vlastos, G. 1953. "Isonomia." *American Journal of Philology* 74:337–366.

Vlastos, G. 1955. "Review of F. M. Cornford: *Principium Sapientiae*." *Gnomon* 27:1–7. (Reprinted in Furley and Allen 1970–75.)

Voegelin, Eric. 1956–87. *Order and History*. 5 vols. Baton Rouge.

Voegelin, Eric. 1968. *Science, Politics and Gnosticism*. Chicago.

Walter, H. 1976. *Das Heraion von Samos*. Munich.

Warmington, E. H. 1934. *Greek Geography*. London.

Illustration Sources

Page xi: From *La Campagna Romana* (Montreal, 1990). Photo courtesy of Geoffrey James, © 1990 by Geoffrey James.

Page 23: From *Di Lucio Vitruvio Pollione de architectura libri decem* (first Italian edition of Vitruvius, translated and illustrated by Cesare Cesariano; Como, 1521), folio CXLIX recto.

Page 26: After J. M. Robinson, *An Introduction to Early Greek Philosophy* (Boston, 1968). Cf. Hurwit 1985, p. 208.

Page 29: Photo courtesy of the Villa Giulia. Reproduced by permission.

Page 30: From William Hamilton, *Painted Greek Vases*, illustrated and explained by James Milligan (London, 1823).

Page 33: From *Di Lucio Vitruvio Pollione de architectura libri decem*, folio CLVII recto.

Page 37: From *Di Lucio Vitruvio Pollione de architectura libri decem*, folio XXVIII recto.

Page 45: Musée du Louvre. Photo: Musées Nationaux, Paris. © Photo R.M.N.

Page 50: From Casson 1991, © Princeton University Press. Reprinted by permission of Princeton University Press.

Page 53: From *Di Lucio Vitruvio Pollione de architectura libri decem*, folio XXIII recto.

Page 61: From Jacques Ier Androuet du Cerceau, *Les plus excellents bastiments de France* (1576 and 1579).

Page 65: Oxford, Ashmolean Museum (1922-208). Photo: Ashmolean Museum. Reproduced by permission.

Page 69: From J. Baudoin, *Recueils d'emblèmes divers* (Paris, 1638), pp. 114, 362.

Page 85: After Martin 1974.

Page 87: After Adam 1982.

Page 90: Photo courtesy of the trustees of the British Museum.

Page 94: The Metropolitan Museum of Art, New York, purchase 1942, Joseph Pulitzer Bequest (42.11.21). Photo: Metropolitan Museum of Art.

Page 100: After Walter 1976.

Page 103: After Bervé, Gruben, and Hirmer n.d.

Page 105: Musée du Louvre. Photo: Musées Nationaux, Paris. © Photo R.M.N.

Page 108: The Metropolitan Museum of Art, New York, Fletcher Fund, 1931 (31.11.10). Photo: Metropolitan Museum of Art.

Page 113: From *Di Lucio Vitruvio Pollione de architectura libri decem*, folio XXXII recto.

Page 115: Reprinted from Coulton 1977. © 1977 by J. J. Coulton. Used by permission of the publisher, Cornell University Press.

Page 117: Photo: Indra Kagis McEwen.

Page 120: Royal Ontario Museum, Toronto. Gift of Dr. Sigmund Samuel. Photo courtesy of the Royal Ontario Museum. Reproduced by permission.

Page 124: Nineteenth-century engraving by Auguste F. Lemaître. Reprinted from Walter 1976.

Index

Achaeans, 81, 93–95
Achilles, 22, 42, 68, 94
Achilles' shield. *See* Shield of
    Achilles
Acropolis. *See* Athens, Acropolis
Aegeus, 57
Aeolipyles, 52
Aeschylus, 35
  Agamemnon, 35, 60
  Eumenides, 60, 127
Aetos. *See* Pediments
Agamemnon, 60
Agathemerus, 26, 31
Agora, 46, 110, 113, 118
  in Athens, 1, 75
  in Sparta, 74
Aias, 34
Alberti, Leon Battista, 96, 129
Alcinous, 56, 58
Analemma, 38
Anamnēsis, 6. *See also* Memory;
    Recollection
Anaximander of Miletus, 9–38,
    41, 46–48, 51–52, 54, 79,
    123–124
  apeiron of, 10–13, 16, 138n26
    (*see also* ***Apeiros***; ***Aporia***)
  B1 fragment, 10–17, 36, 48,
    52, 124
  celestial globe, 17, 19, 23–25,
    36, 52
  cosmic model, 17–19, 47, 123
    (*see also* ***Gnōmōn***)
  cosmology, 23–25, 47, 124
  father of, 166n14
  map of the world, 17, 19, 25–
    32, 36, 62 (*see also* ***Pinax***)
Apeiron. *See* Anaximander of
    Miletus, ***apeiron*** of

Apeiros, 13, 15–16, 52, 59, 73.
    See also Anaximander of
    Miletus, ***apeiron*** of; ***Aporia***
Aphrodite, 44, 59
Apollo, 88
Apollonia, 9
Aporia, 59–60, 62. *See also*
    Apeiros
Apsides, 24–25. *See also* Wheels
Archaic Greece, 2, 130
Archaion agalma. *See* Athena
    Polias, wooden cult statue of
Archē, 10, 13, 75, 89, 118–119
Arērōs, 51, 53
Ares, 59
Ariadne, 57–58
Ariadne's dance, 58–59, 62–64,
    81, 126
Aristagoras of Miletus, 27–28,
    31–32
Aristotle, 11, 75
  Metaphysics, 125
  Physics, 9, 82 (*see also*
    Simplicius)
  Politics, 87
Armor, 24, 48, 53. *See also*
    Shields
Artifact and ***kosmos***. *See* ***Kosmos***,
    artifact and
Artisan, 42, 75. *See also*
    Craftsmen; ***Dēmiourgos***
Athena, 22, 34, 44, 56, 88–89,
    93–94
  birth of, 127
  owl of, 91, 93
  peplos of, 89–93 (*see also*
    Peplos)
  Phidias' colossal statue of, 91,
    116

Athena Polias, wooden cult
statue of, 91–92, 96
Athens, 1, 57, 81, 84, 95
Acropolis, 1, 79, 93, 114, 116
evacuation of, 96–97
hegemony of, 128
Mycenaean citadel of, 79, 89,
91, 95
political decline of, 97
sea power of, 86, 96–97

Babylonians, 19, 33
Becoming, 41, 83
Being, 15, 125–126
Great Chain of, 51
Birth, 20, 71, 127. *See also*
Genesis
Black Sea, 79
Boats. *See* Ships
Body, Homeric, 43, 49, 55,
146n12. *See also **Chrōs**;*
Soma
Bonds. *See **Apeiros**;* Bound
statues
Boundless, the. *See* Anaximander
of Miletus, ***apeiron*** of;
Apeiros
Bound statues, 1, 4–6, 56, 101,
116–118. *See also **Xoana***
Browning, Robert, 70

Calypso, 28, 49
Carpentry, 48, 128. *See also*
Ships, construction of
Casson, Lionel, 49–50, 71, 96
Cave, 127, 156n20
Celestial globe. *See* Anaximander
of Miletus, celestial globe

Cerameicus, 92–93
Chalkeia, 91
Chaos, 60, 70. *See also **Chaos***
Chaos, 11, 60–64, 82. *See also*
Chaos
Chersiphron, 102
Chōra, 81–83, 89, 91
Choros, 2, 44, 57–64, 74, 91–93
Chōros. *See **Chōra***
Chreōn. *See* Custom; Necessity
Christians, 55
Chronos, 10, 15–16, 38, 64,
137n23. *See also **Gnōmōn**;*
Time, order of
Chrōs, 43–44, 71. *See also* Body,
Homeric
Chthonie, 54, 70
Cimon, 96
City founders, 110
City-state. *See **Polis***
Civic harmony, 129–130. *See also*
Kosmos, political
Cleomenes, 27, 31–32
Clytemnestra, 60
Coldstream, J. N., 99
Colonization, 9, 76, 80, 94–95,
110
Colonnades. *See* Columns; ***Pteron**;*
Temples, peripteral
Column drums, 19, 26–27, 123–
124. *See also* Anaximander
of Miletus, cosmology;
Earth, shape of
Columns, 99–100, 111–112,
119–120. *See also **Pteron**;*
Temples, peripteral
Community, 72, 113. *See also*
Civic harmony; Craft and
community